CREATING COMMUNITY

T0288353

CREATING COMMUNITY

Life and Learning at Montgomery's Black University

Edited by
KARL E. WESTHAUSER, ELAINE M. SMITH,
AND JENNIFER A. FREMLIN

THE UNIVERSITY OF ALABAMA PRESS
Tuscaloosa

Typeface: AGaramond

∞

The paper on which this book is printed meets the minimum requirements of American
National Standard for Information Science—Permanence of Paper for Printed Library
Materials, ANSI Z39.48-1984.

Library of Congress Cataloging-in-Publication Data

Creating community : life and learning at Montgomery's Black university / edited by
Karl E. Westhauser, Elaine M. Smith, and Jennifer A. Fremlin.
p. cm.
Includes bibliographical references and index.
ISBN 0-8173-1463-6 (cloth : alk. paper)
ISBN 10: 0-8173-5499-9 (pbk. : alk. paper)
ISBN 13: 978-0-8173-5499-2 (pbk. : alk. paper)
1. Alabama State University—History. 2. Alabama State University—Faculty—Anecdotes.
3. African American universities and colleges—Alabama—Montgomery—History.
I. Westhauser, Karl E. (Karl Edwin), 1961– II. Smith, Elaine M., 1942– III. Fremlin,
Jennifer A. (Jennifer Anne), 1962–
LD59.A53C74 2005
378.761′47—dc22

2004029032

The essay by Jennifer A. Fremlin was first published in *The Chronicle of Higher Education*'s
online Careers section, December 11, 2002.

Contents

Photographs follow page 88

Preface

The essays in this volume were generated by a suggestion that we, the editors, made to our colleagues in the Department of Humanities at Alabama State University: to write personal essays on their experiences at ASU that, when taken together, might illuminate some of the institution's hidden assets. The various faculty who responded interpreted the charge on their own terms, but in coming together, the collection as a whole resulted in a cohesive project. Out of their many voices, one constant theme emerged: that of community, specifically the community that each found on arrival at ASU, and that each in turn contributed to. While most university departments are likely heterogeneous in their mix of faculty and students, we quickly realized that not only did the collection attest to the strength of a unique community at this institution, but was itself produced out of the particular social and historical circumstances of the historically black university (see Introduction). Alabama State University's location in the center of Montgomery and its particular institutional formation are intimately related to the history of civil rights in the South. Yet the personal nature of the accounts challenges readers to see today's black university not just as a historic institution, but also as a vital, living community.

The faculty members who introduce themselves here are broadly representative of the faculty in the Department of Humanities, at ASU, and at historically black colleges and universities (HBCUs) generally in that they are a remarkably diverse group of people. Diversity has always been one of the hallmarks of HBCUs, in part because they have always accepted white Americans and people from around the world, even when predominantly white institutions maintained rigid barriers against diversity. Such "minorities" already account for over forty percent of HBCU faculty, even as many predominantly white institutions still struggle to diversify their campuses. While the number and diversity of minority faculty contribute much to today's black university, the diversity of its African American *majority* has always been a proud badge of distinction. Making the most of the human potential squandered by white America, the black university continues to draw to itself black faculty, as well as students, from all across the nation. Majority and minority faculty members alike bring to the black university a valuable diversity of life experiences, including expertise acquired from an impressive cross-section of degree-granting graduate and undergraduate institutions, both historically black and predominantly white, at home and abroad. Together, they help to foster a degree of cosmopolitanism both enjoyable and stimulating.

The essays are grouped according to aspects of this theme of a shared community, recognizing the regional and racial diversities that have come together. The first section, "Alabama: Black-White Mix," includes accounts by three native Alabamians, two African American and one white, of their respective experiences growing up and working in the Heart of Dixie. Kathy Dunn Jackson's essay, "You Can Go Home Again," details the haven that Alabama State's campus provided her, the daughter of a professor for whom a campus dormitory is now named, in the heart of segregated 1950s Montgomery, as she literally grew up on the grounds of the college. Although she left the university to head north, first to Fisk University in Nashville, Tennessee, and then to the University of Michigan, no one was more surprised than she when she returned to Alabama to finish her studies at the state's flagship land-grant institution and went on to spend her teaching and administrative career at ASU. Virginia Jones's account in "E Pluribus Unum" of growing up white in Birmingham during the sixties relates her growing consciousness of how race affected her understanding of her home. She struggles with the dilemma posed by living in a culture she loves, increasingly at odds with its violent response to the shifting racial climate. In "Genesis of the National Center for the Study of Civil Rights and African-American Culture," Janice R. Franklin, a native daughter who graduated from perhaps the most fabled of all black universities, Booker T. Washington's Tuskegee Institute, outlines the recent founding at ASU of a nationally significant site for studying civil rights history, appropriately enough on the campus where many of the struggle's events had their inception.

The second section, "Region-Wide: Seamless Fit," broadens the book's scope from the community found by those already in the state of Alabama to the regional South. In coming to Alabama, and in one case coming back, these three authors find ways in which their experience at ASU is enriched by their participation in other institutions. In the tradition of educational autobiography, Frank E. Moorer's account in "I Go to College" highlights firsthand the significance of historically black institutions to his educational and personal development. Born in rural Alabama, Moorer struggled to gain his education, and as he demonstrates, it was the mission of HBCUs—Oakwood College, Selma University, Rust College, and Atlanta University specifically—that helped him attain his goal. Elaine M. Smith graduated from her native Florida's Bethune-Cookman College, a private black college founded and long guided by Mary McLeod Bethune, with whom she became acquainted and on whose career she has since become the foremost academic authority. Her arrival as an adult in Montgomery from Florida was punctuated by her involvement in several women's organizations, as she relates in "Living a Womanist Legacy." And Annie P. Markham, who graduated from Jackson State University in her native Mississippi, where legendary Margaret Walker Alexander filled her with inspiration, landed at ASU when her husband became head coach of the football team. She finds opportunity not only on the campus, but also in melding it productively with the church experience afforded her in Montgomery, as she attests in "I Pledge Allegiance to My 'Black-Eyed Susan' University." These three southerners find Alabama culturally distinct yet in the end, through ASU's intervention, hospitable.

ASU houses not only southerners in its midst, but like most HBCUs is made up of faculty from across the nation. In the third section, "Non-Southern: What Difference?" two midwesterners and a northeasterner find themselves teaching in the Deep South, and the experience profoundly affects each of them. Robert Ely revisits events in his life growing up in Indiana from the perspective of relocating to Alabama in "Portrait of the Artist as a Young White Man." Like others of his generation, he already embodied a significant transformation that was then changing the nation as a whole. It is only through the experience of teaching at a black university for the past twenty-five years that Ely, a white liberal from the heartland, finds himself truly transformed. Karl E. Westhauser, a European historian from New York, learns more about history from the "City on a Hill" and teaching in the context of a black university than he could have predicted, and the experience profoundly shapes his perspective. And Missouri-born and -raised Margaret Holler Stephens, the daughter of a German immigrant father, feels "Called Home" to Alabama. A journalist before becoming a teacher, she finds that it is the spirit of community at this black university that fosters dialogue, which she believes is a right of free people and a means to progress.

Finally, two non-American faculty members, a Canadian and an Indian, add their voices to the sense of belonging that others have found at Alabama State University. In the fourth section, "International: All Welcome," Jennifer A. Fremlin illustrates in her essay "'You're Not White, You're Canadian': Where I Belong," how ASU made her feel welcome in Montgomery, incongruously both the "Cradle of the Confederacy" and the birthplace of the modern civil rights movement, where she at first felt herself to be very much an outsider. Sunita George, who is from a Christian minority in her native India, muses on the similarities and differences of minority experience that working at ASU has taught her in "The Color Brown: An Asian's Perspective." These international faculty members feel at home at ASU because they find it to be a community that is not only diverse but also highly accepting of individuals' differences.

In an Afterword, noted sociologist John Moland Jr. puts some of these individual experiences in a more schematic perspective, noting that their responses and testimonies to the sense of community that each respondent has found at Alabama State University are not accidental; indeed, it is because ASU is a historically black institution located in Montgomery, Alabama, that each has found, together, the unique and special community that is their collective home. For too long, the HBCU's role in American culture has been neglected, and its most valuable, human assets may have been overlooked. Montgomery's black university possesses many such assets, including those who have contributed essays to this volume. These voices rise together to attest to the transformative role of this institution in each of their lives, and in so doing demonstrate the ways in which each works towards its continual renewal.

The individual's transformation begins with a warm welcome, an uplifting spirit of community that brings out the best in faculty members and others, extending a proud tradition. Such work tends to call forth a strong commitment, from faculty members and others. When new individuals become part of this community, as faculty or as students, they may experience a radical transformation, coming to see themselves and their relationships with others in a different light. The black university is today, as it has always been, a diverse community built through the combined efforts of many different individuals working together every day, bridging differences and negotiating commonalities. "All feel welcome" at the black university, Fremlin writes—"all, that is, who value human experience and achievement."

To be sure, Montgomery's black university holds no monopoly on any of these assets, taken individually: one will find experiences of diversity or commitment, transformation or community on other campuses across the United States, in some combination and to some degree. But the black university possesses every one of these assets and possesses them all in abundance. They are part and parcel of the legacy of African American history and culture. Taken together, they foster a distinctive vision of shared humanity and produce a unique range of educational experiences. Such a vision and such experiences are particularly valuable today. Today's black university not only preserves the past but also ensures that we may learn from it, teaching lessons vital to a successful future.

⌒

This volume is a tribute to countless individuals—faculty, staff, students, administrators, alumni, and other friends of Alabama State University—who over the years helped to create the community which it describes. It is also the product of the academics who came together to write it. We are deeply indebted to them, for they demonstrated uncommon courage and honesty in revealing personal dimensions of their public careers and upheld high standards of professionalism that made our work more pleasurable than we had a right to expect. We are particularly grateful to Kathy Dunn Jackson for sharing not only memories of growing up on the ASU campus but also photographs of those days, which are included in this volume. We thank Virginia M. Jones, Chair of the Department of Humanities when this project was conceived, for unconditional and unwavering enthusiasm. We also thank John Moland Jr. for reading and commenting on the draft manuscript and allowing us to include his analysis in the volume.

Alabama State University also provided essential institutional and financial support for this project. We gratefully acknowledge Joe A. Lee, President of Alabama State University; Evelyn White, Vice President for Academic Affairs; T. Clifford Bibb, Dean of University College; and David Iyegha, Chair of the Department of Humanities. We thank Alfred S. Smith, Assistant Vice President for Academic Affairs for his counsel and endorsement.

We also thank Rebecca Mohr, Head Circulation Librarian, and other staff of the Levi Watkins Learning Center, for their assistance; the former Office of Communications and Public Affairs, under John F. Knight Jr., for generous recognition and publicity for our efforts; and David Campbell, University Photographer, for expert assistance. William H. Harris, past president of Alabama State University, has our appreciation for encouraging us at the time of the project's inception.

Several forums offered contributors valuable opportunities to present and refine works-in-progress. At ASU, forums were sponsored by the Department of Humanities and the Steering Committee for the Inauguration of President Joe A. Lee. Other presentations were delivered at the Orlando meeting of the Association for the Study of African American Life and History (ASALH) and the Southern Conference on African American Studies, Inc. (SCAASI) meetings in San Antonio, Charleston, and Nashville.

Our greatest debts beyond the ASU community are to the staff of the University of Alabama Press and their director, who took an early interest in the project, coming to ASU to meet with us and promote the Press among other interested faculty members; to the Press's anonymous reviewers, whose thoughtful critiques helped to enhance our vision for the volume; and to the individuals who patiently and diligently guided this project to fruition.

Behind the scenes, friends and family provided loving support and capable assistance when needed, which was often. Karon S. Bailey, Elizabeth M. Johnson, Dorothy B. LaSaine, John T. LaSaine Jr., Lise Westhauser, and Steve Willoughby all provided helpful evaluations of our work at key stages. For instilling in us values that continue to sustain us, we gratefully acknowledge our parents.

At every stage, we as editors shared together all aspects of this project as true and faithful partners. We complemented each other with respect to our gifts, temperaments, and areas of expertise. We learned from each other.

Karl E. Westhauser
Elaine M. Smith
Jennifer A. Fremlin

Introduction

The community described in this volume is a diverse one that includes blacks and whites, women and men, the native-born and immigrants from around the world. It is representative of American society and a product of the American dream. That dream has always promised freedom and opportunity, and these are what higher education has come to represent—the opportunity to free oneself through intellectual growth, through social or economic advancement, through career and job satisfaction, or all of these. Today, the United States can boast of approximately one hundred and eighteen historically black colleges and universities (HBCUs) amongst its several thousand institutions of higher education—all helping to make the American dream a reality. Alabama State University (ASU), a historically black university located in Montgomery, Alabama, is one of them.

ASU situates itself within the historic tradition of American higher education, recently commemorated in the ceremonies for the inauguration of Joe A. Lee as ASU's eleventh president in April 2003. On that occasion, ASU's president received greetings from the president of Harvard University brought by a delegate who was, in turn, invited to lead a procession of representatives of other institutions and of ASU's own faculty. These gestures of mutual respect demonstrate ASU's participation in a tradition dating back to the founding of America's first institution of higher education, Harvard University, in 1636. The ideals that this tradition represents are part of the inspiration for this volume, as they are for all faculty members who work to contribute to the sum of human knowledge and experience. Like good faculty everywhere, ASU's faculty members seek to contribute to the expansion and preservation of "Veritas" (Truth), which is the motto of Harvard University, and to graduate students "qualify'd for Discharging the Offices of Life with usefulness and reputation," as the 1764 charter of Brown University put it (Brown University 74). Such ideals, vital to American higher education since its early days, remain vital to the community described in this volume.

Yet education was not a key part of the American dream in the two centuries after the first English settlements were established. The majority of America's children received little education and only a select few—economically privileged white men—ever went on to higher education. Most Americans, white as well as black, were effectively excluded. Unlike any other group, the vast majority of African Americans were reduced to slavery, systematically denied the fundamental right to freedom as well as to opportunity and education. The first laws establishing the supremacy of "white over black" in the North American colonies were written in Massachusetts in the 1640s (Jordan ix). Accordingly, connections between education, freedom, and opportunity emerge particularly clearly in the history of black America. The distinctive aspirations and contributions of African Americans were, and still are, embodied in the development of black schools, colleges, and universities, such as ASU. The historical development of ASU has been part of the historical development of a society that brings education within the reach of all, regardless of race, gender, economic circumstance, or national origin.

Creating Community: Freedom and Education, ca. 1630–ca. 1950

A good part of the inspiration for the foundation and expansion of American educational institutions has come from religious conviction. The pilgrims and Puritans who settled Massachusetts believed that Christian boys and girls should be taught to read so that each might read the Bible. Harvard University was founded to train ministers for the church and Brown University's Baptist roots are still evident today in its motto, "In Deo Speramus"—In God We Trust. The year of independence, 1776, saw the founding of the nation's first collegiate honor society, Phi Beta Kappa, but only nine institutions of higher education had been established, all for men only and all but one, Virginia's College of William and Mary, in the North. By that time, the northern colonies had mandated that localities designate public funds to establish and maintain schools for children, but such laws were not well enforced. The southern colonies had not much concerned themselves with educational institutions, preferring to leave the schooling of children largely to the parents, few of whom were able or willing to pay for it (Button and Provenzo 14–15, 21; Norton et al. 47, 88–89; Meyer et al. 41).

African Americans were among the first to fight and die during the war for national independence, but the revolution did not abolish slavery. To be sure, there were perhaps 59,000 free blacks in America, living mostly in the northern port cities of New York and Philadelphia. But there were almost twelve times that number of slaves, all of them black and almost all of them living in the South (Bennett 77). Throughout the South, it was a criminal offense to teach a slave to read (Button and Provenzo 141). A few African Americans were taught and learned to read anyway, as the great colonial poet Phillis Wheatley demonstrated. Unlike black children, white girls were expected to learn to read, but colleges were closed to women. White women who pursued intellectual development on their own found no careers open to them, no economic opportunity, a bleak prospect that loomed throughout the following century (Button and Provenzo 140). Moreover, "free" women of whatever color had no right to vote.

Nevertheless, linkages between freedom and education became more marked. Beginning with Vermont in 1777, the northern states soon abolished slavery and free blacks set up some of the first new schools in the new nation. They did so on their own initiative and with the help of white religious and philanthropic organizations. The first schools for blacks were set up in Philadelphia by Richard Allen, in Boston by Prince Hall, and in New York City by the New York Manumission Society. Established in 1787, New York's Free African Schools marked the beginning of free secular education in that state. Twenty years later, former slaves opened the first black school in the nation's capital (Bennett 83, 172). The newly free nation asserted a national interest in education through the Old Northwest Territory Land Ordinances of 1785 and 1787, which mandated that a set portion of the public land then being settled beyond the Appalachians was to be set aside for the support of free public education (Button and Provenzo 71). Despite such advances, blacks and black schools encountered much hostility in the northern states. Yet the contrast between north and south grew more marked as slavery not only persisted but also expanded in the South. The South also increasingly distinguished itself from the rest of the nation by its disinterest in funding public education and public welfare generally, even as southern legislatures duly chartered state institutions of higher education, including the University of Alabama, which opened its doors in 1831 (Meyer et al. 48; University of Alabama 1).

In higher education, there were signs of growing opportunity for white women and African Americans. The first colleges for women were established by Mary Lyon, who opened Troy Seminary in Troy, New York, in 1821 and by Emma Willard, who opened Mt. Holyoke Female Seminary in Massachusetts in 1836. Three years later, Massachusetts established the nation's first state teacher-training high school, called a "normal school" (Button and Provenzo 138, 118). The first black colleges were founded in Pennsylvania by the Quakers, the only Christian sect that had never accepted slavery. The oldest of these, Cheyney University of Pennsylvania, was founded in 1837 (Bennett 172–73, 457). Not all education of blacks and women was separate. The first black known to have graduated from an American institution of higher education received his degree from Middlebury College, in Vermont, in 1823. There would be other blacks who would gain admission to various colleges in Massachusetts, New Hampshire, New Jersey, and other northern states. Oberlin College, in Ohio, began admitting women along with men in 1833 (Button and Provenzo 143; Meyer et al. 49). Despite these signs of change, the landscape of higher education changed little for the vast majority of Americans. While the number of colleges, like the number of schools, continued to grow apace with the nation, not more than one boy in two hundred would ever attend college in the early 1800s (Button and Provenzo 82).

The Civil War (1861–1865) extended the promise of freedom and the hope of the American dream to black Americans who for centuries had been denied basic human rights and dignity. Once prohibited from learning the alphabet, former slaves demonstrated an enthusiasm for education that exceeded that of whites at the time (Litwack 53). Serving this vast new population of students, of all ages, brought about what was probably the single greatest expansion of educational institutions in American history. Already in 1861, the first day school for freedmen was founded in Virginia, with a black teacher; the following year, dozens of white teachers from New England were ferried to the sea islands of South Carolina and Georgia by one of Lincoln's generals (Bennett 466; Button and Provenzo 143). At every opportunity, blacks founded and began operating their own schools, usually with the help of northern white teachers, churches, and philanthropic organizations, such as the American Missionary Association, as well as, for a short time, the federal Freedman's Bureau. The founding of the South's first black colleges, Atlanta University and Virginia Union, came in 1865, the year that saw the end of the war and the abolition of slavery with ratification of the Thirteenth Amendment to the Constitution. While black colleges at first offered what was essentially secondary education, Howard University, founded in the nation's capital in 1866, offered college-level courses from its inception (Button and Provenzo 144).

The Civil War brought white Americans educational gains as well, through the expansion of federal funding for higher education. Authorized by the Morrill Act of 1862, this program had been blocked by the opposition of socially conservative southerners until the election of Lincoln and the secession of the southern states cleared the way (Parsons 29; Norton et al. 370). The Morrill Act granted federal land to the states to generate funds for institutions of higher education, effectively extending the idea of the Old Northwest Land Acts to the rest of the nation. It specified that land-grant funds were to be used to establish colleges in the new areas of agriculture and engineering, thereby spurring the further development of the higher education curriculum. Ultimately, the Act fostered sixty-nine colleges and universities, including Cornell University, a private endowed institution designated the land-grant institution of New York State, whose founder affirmed new ideals of diversity and inclusiveness by declaring in 1865, "I would found an institution where any person can find instruction in any study." In the South, new public "Agricultural and Mechanical" colleges emerged, including today's Auburn University, a failed private white institution that was designated the A&M College of Alabama when taken over by the state in 1872 (Norton et al. 394–95; Button and Provenzo 155–56, 304; Cornell University 1; Auburn University 1).

Alabama State University is one of the fruits of the great expansion of freedom and opportunity brought by the Civil War. The university was founded in 1867 as Lincoln Normal School in Marion, Alabama, by nine black men—Alexander H. Curtis, Joey Pinch, Thomas Speed, Nickolas Dale, James Childs, Thomas Lee, John Freeman, Nathan Levert and David Harris (Caver 30–32). These "Marion Nine" enlisted the support of the American Missionary Association (AMA), which supplied the white teachers and raised contributions from the Freedman's Bureau, the black community, and, after 1870, the state of Alabama. In 1874, after the first elected black member of the state board of education, Peyton Finley, persuaded the state legislature to establish America's first state-supported educational institution for blacks, the school's first president, George N. Card, who was also black, reorganized the school as "State Normal School and University for the Education of Colored Teachers and Students." In 1887, State Normal School and University moved to Montgomery under the leadership of a white president, William Burns Paterson, a Scotsman, and his wife, Maggie, an Oberlin graduate and missionary teacher. They and nine white AMA faculty members held classes in Beulah Baptist Church until 1903, when the school erected its first building on land donated by Montgomery's black community. When the long-serving Paterson died in 1915, he was succeeded by the man he had hired as the institution's first black teacher, John William Beverly. Normal School began offering college-level courses leading to the bachelor's degree in 1928 and became Teachers College in 1929 (Paterson 14; "Alabama State University: The History").

By the early twentieth century, all of the elements of today's public education system had been established. City public school systems, along with city, county, and state school superintendents, had emerged across the nation and suited the needs of the industrialized society that had emerged. After 1900, child and adolescent employment declined and school enrollment and attendance increased, with over ninety percent of all children between the ages of five and seventeen attending school in 1926 (Meyer et al. 62; Button and Provenzo 113, 115, 210). Increased public funding for education was distributed along racial lines, with state and local appropriations to white institutions far outstripping those to black institutions. A second Morrill Act (1890) required states receiving land-grant funds to establish equal institutions for blacks if they insisted on maintaining separate ones for whites (Parsons 30). Today's Alabama A&M University, founded in 1875 as a black institution in Normal, Alabama, was designated that state's land-grant institution for blacks as a result. Although the principle of "separate but equal" was upheld by the Supreme Court, equality never materialized.

For every accredited high school for blacks before the Depression, there were twenty-five for whites (Button and Provenzo 303–4).

By the early twentieth century, black colleges had come to stand at the center of black communities led by the cadres of skilled and professional men and women they had educated. In 1895, Booker T. Washington, one of the first graduates of Hampton Institute (now Hampton University), emerged as a singularly powerful spokesman for black Americans. Seeing "industrial" education as the key to increasing economic prosperity for the black community as a whole, he founded perhaps the most famous of all black colleges, Tuskegee Institute, with this purpose in 1881 (Bennett 328). He not only disagreed with William Paterson's belief in equal education but also competed for the same state tax dollars and did his best to prevent Normal School from relocating to the state capital (Paterson 16; Harlan 166–67). In the year Normal School became Teachers College (1929) the most famous of all African American leaders, Martin Luther King Jr., was born in the relatively prosperous black community of "Sweet Auburn" in Atlanta, Georgia. Like his father and grandfather before him, he graduated from Morehouse College (1948) and, like them, took up a career in the ministry. He chose to pursue a doctorate, and, like others in the growing ranks of black college graduates, went north to do so because the segregated system of education denied blacks equal opportunity in the South ("Martin Luther King" 1).

For those who could afford tuition, the early twentieth century was in many ways the classic age of American higher education. The number of students multiplied in the expanding, industrializing economy, from 52,000 in 1870 to 600,000 by 1920, while the institutions available to accommodate them grew from 563 in 1870 to nearly a thousand in 1900 (Norton et al. 597, 599). The National Collegiate Athletic Association was formed in 1905, in response to the new popularity of men's football, while the number of women in higher education continued to grow, nearly matching the number of men by 1920. In that year, ratification of the Nineteenth Amendment gave women the right to vote (Norton 548–49, 598). By 1945, the college man had cornered the market on professional and management positions; the college woman usually chose marriage and children over career and graduate study (Button and Provenzo 285). Betty Friedan gave up a graduate fellowship when her prospective husband asked her to choose between them; Coretta Scott completed her graduate program at the Boston Conservatory of Music but did not pursue the singing career she had planned. Instead, she chose to become a partner in the ministry of her new husband, Martin Luther King Jr. (Friedan 70; Galegroup 1).

The early twentieth century also saw the spread of the Progressive belief that the goal of education was to remake society. Thomas Dewey asserted that schools should promote social progress by serving as community centers that prepared children for productive citizenship (Norton et al. 596). New "social scientists," historians, and lawyers focused on applying academic research to social progress. The first black PhD from Harvard, sociologist W. E. B. Du Bois, became an activist professor at Atlanta University. As a founding member of the National Association for the Advancement of Colored People (NAACP) in 1909 and editor of its magazine *The Crisis* until 1934, DuBois spent decades rallying opposition to racial segregation and the denial of blacks' voting rights. Black militancy spread along with black advances in education and prosperity and service in two world wars. NAACP membership skyrocketed from 50,000 in 1940 to 450,000 in 1946 (Norton et al. 803). That same year, women in Montgomery, Alabama, organized the Women's Political Council (WPC) to "elevate" the consciousness of the city's black population. Many members of the WPC belonged to the campus community of Alabama State University (then Teachers College) and professor Mary Fair Burks, chair of the English department, was the organization's founding president (Robinson 22–23).

Creating Community: Equal Opportunity, Since ca. 1950

The mass movement of black Americans for freedom to exercise their Constitutional rights, something white Americans mostly take for granted, won famous victories with the passage of the Civil Rights Act of 1964 and the Voting Rights Acts of 1965. Also passed in 1965 were the Elementary and Secondary Education Act and the Higher Education Act. These acts made education the lynchpin of a new American dream, the Great Society, which would set aside a share of the nation's resources to give all Americans better opportunity to make the most of their lives.

Public education was the focus of a revolutionary campaign against segregation launched by the NAACP Legal Defense and Educational Fund in 1950. Under the direction of Thurgood Marshall, a product of Lincoln University of Pennsylvania and Howard University School of Law, NAACP lawyers won victories for black graduate school students in Texas and Oklahoma. The following year, they filed complaints against segregated elementary and secondary school systems on behalf of plaintiffs in Delaware, Kansas, South Carolina, Virginia, and Washington, D.C. Under *Brown v. Board of Education of Topeka, Kansas,* the U.S. Supreme Court ruled unanimously that segregation in public education was unconstitutional and, in 1955, ordered the schools desegregated "with all deliberate speed." When white reaction in Mississippi, Kentucky, and Tennessee erupted in mobs, murders, and the dynamiting of an elementary school, black Americans launched a mass movement of militant nonviolence (Bennett 374–77). Martin Luther King Jr., the new pastor of the Dexter Avenue Baptist Church in Montgomery, Alabama, was asked to lead the boycott of the city's segregated buses that began on Monday, December 5, 1955. The Cradle of the Confederacy thus became the Birthplace of the Modern Civil Rights Movement.

Faculty at black colleges took leading roles in the civil rights movement. It started at Alabama State University (then Alabama State College) on Thursday, December 1, 1955, after Rosa Parks became the second woman to be arrested on the city buses. ASC professor Jo Ann Robinson, president of the Women's Political Council since 1950, knew that the moment black women had long anticipated had arrived and laid out her thinking to Parks's attorney, Fred Gray, an ASC alumnus (Robinson 43–45; Gray 50–52). She spent the night hammering out a notice urging black riders to stay off the buses on Monday and clandestinely copied over fifty thousand flyers on college paper and equipment, abetted by two male students and a male faculty member with a key to the copy room (Robinson 45–46). As soon as a busy schedule of Friday classes permitted, WPC members distributed the notices throughout the community, by which time a meeting at the Dexter Avenue church had selected King to inspire the masses and scheduled a mass meeting for Monday night, to conclude what all hoped would be the boycott's first successful day (Robinson 46–47, 53–56; King, *Stride,* 44–46). Two months later, ASC student (and mother of four) Aurelia Shines Browder consented to let Gray name her lead plaintiff in the lawsuit, *Browder v. Gayle,* that would desegregate the buses and end the boycott in December 1956 (Gray 69–70). By then, other black college towns had started bus boycotts, including Atlanta, Georgia, and Tallahassee, Florida (Bennett 379).

In 1960, students at black colleges started a new phase of the civil rights movement by taking action on their own initiative. It began on February 1, when four North Carolina A&T students sat down at a whites-only lunch counter in a Woolworth's store in Greensboro, North Carolina. Students at other schools followed their example, leading to the birth of the Student Nonviolent Coordinating Committee (SNCC) two months later (Bennett 383–84). In Montgomery, twenty-nine ASC students staged a sit-in at the lunch counter of the county courthouse on February 25th and over a thousand others supported them in a demonstration on the steps of the state capitol five days later. A furious Governor John Patterson forced the expulsion of nine students and the dismissal of more than a dozen ASC faculty, including Jo Ann Robinson and WPC founding president Mary Fair Burks. Knowing that their annual contracts would not be renewed, they left ASC quietly at the end of the term; only history professor Lawrence Reddick departed under protest. ASC president Harper Councill Trenholm succumbed to illness, was replaced, and died on February 20, 1962. Three months later, the expelled students were vindicated by the U.S. Supreme Court, which let stand a ruling that they had been denied their Constitutional right to due process. The decision, *Dixon v. Alabama State Board of Education,* is considered a landmark ruling in higher education (Watkins 28–30, 35–37, 55, 39).

Out of the struggles and sacrifices of the civil rights movement came the Great Society, the new American dream, but it was not what King had dreamed in his speech from the Lincoln Memorial during the March on Washington in 1963 (Bennett 406–7). King dreamed of "black and white together." What would emerge was government machinery to help manage infringements on the rights of others—and continuing racism. King dreamed of all God's children joining hands. What would emerge was a minority rainbow coalition and competing lists of demands from groups too often intent on labeling and relabeling themselves and others. By 1968, King also dreamed of guaranteed employment and a guaranteed livable income for every American (Bennett 428). What had already emerged were massive federal financial assistance programs, some for the middle class as well as the poor, programs that would set the stage for perennial struggles over taxes, budgets, and blame. With dazzling skill and speed, President Lyndon Johnson had moved through Congress over seventy pieces of Great Society legislation which, together, created the new American dream (Norton et al. 946). The nation's leaders achieved an epochal national compromise not unlike independence in 1776 or abolition in 1865. Many Americans, black as well as white, turned to the business of making the most of it. By 1970, the nation's black revolution had spent itself (Bennett 433).

The Great Society put into action the Progressive belief that education was the key to transforming society by peaceful means. For the first time, America's government used education in the name of social equality, making it a weapon in the War on Poverty. The Economic Opportunity Act of 1964 and the Elementary and Secondary Education Act (ESEA) of 1965 created today's programs for children of low-income families, such as Project Head Start, to prepare preschoolers for grade school, and Upward Bound, for high school students who aspired to a college education. The ESEA also established funds for school libraries and textbooks. College work-study, created by the Equal Opportunities Commission (EOC), was also included in the Higher Education Act (HEA) of 1965—the nation's first general program of federal aid to higher education. Title IV of the HEA created the first federally funded college scholarship program based on need, transformed in 1972 into the Basic Educational Opportunity Grant program and later renamed in honor of its sponsor, Senator Claiborne Pell (Norton et al. 946–47; Parsons 37–38, 50, 59). Title IV also created the first federally guaranteed student loan program. It served to quell opposition to need-based grants by those claiming that students who could not be expected to repay loans were not good enough for scholarships. Initially needed to ensure the bill's passage, the student loan program has, since 1978, been repeatedly expanded, in part by allowing the middle class to participate (Parsons 38, 34, 58). It has thus remained part of the compromise that the Great Society represents.

Thanks to educational and civil rights legislation won by the civil rights movement, America provides far more individuals far more opportunity than ever before to make the most of their lives. Far more Americans enroll in college and receive college degrees than ever before. In 1954, there were only about 100,000 black students attending college and over ninety percent of them were enrolled at black institutions. By the 1980s, predominantly white institutions enrolled nearly eighty percent of black students, whose numbers had jumped to 1.2 million, with nearly forty percent of African Americans between the ages of 18 and 24 enrolling in college in 1997 (Roebuck and Murty 43; Freeman 8; Jackson 29). Black public institutions have seen white student enrollment increase and several had majority white enrollments as early as 1965 (McGrath 13; Roebuck and Murty 43). Students in wheelchairs are provided equal opportunity through building modifications and there are now services for students with learning disabilities. Institutions responded to demands from students involved in the civil rights movement and subsequent liberation movements of women and gay people by creating courses and academic programs in African American studies, women's studies, and gay studies. Title IX of the HEA Amendments of 1972 required that women's sports receive equal funding (Button and Provenzo 300; Mayberry 1–7; Norton et al. 958–61).

While the civil rights movement and Great Society legislation focused on increasing equal opportunity for individual students, they also increased support for black institutions themselves. While black and white institutions were once accredited separately by segregated organizations, an integrated Southern Association of Colleges and Schools (SACS) began accrediting black schools and colleges in 1957. ASC won SACS accreditation in 1966 and, after its name was changed to Alabama State University in 1969, was accredited at the university level in 1970 (Roebuck and Murty 42; Watkins 108, 110). Urban renewal grants from the new Department of Housing and Urban Development enabled Alabama State University to erect twelve new buildings in the late 1960s and early 1970s (Watkins 98–99). Through Title III of the HEA, the federal government established aid to all "developing" institutions of higher education, with black institutions in mind. Alabama State University was granted an independent Board of Trustees by the Alabama legislature in 1975, having previously been governed by the state's board of education. When, in 1986, further legislature required a majority of trustees to hold the bachelor's degree from ASU, the governing board became majority black (Watkins 16, 193, 201–2).

Black institutions must now compete with white institutions in all areas, including faculty. With integration, black faculty became a presence on white campuses all across the nation. At ASC, integration of faculty and staff began in 1967 as a result of a federal court order issued in *Lee v. Macon* that applied to all public institutions of education under the state of Alabama board of education (Watkins 65). ASU's dismissal, in 1972, of a probationary white male faculty member without giving cause and contrary to the department chair's recommendation caused a claim of racial discrimination that was upheld by federal court judge Frank Johnson in 1978 (Watkins 206, 224–25). Today, ASU's faculty, like that of other black institutions, is among the most racially diverse in the nation, far outstripping predominantly white institutions, with non-black faculty accounting for over forty percent. America's production of black PhD's is slowly rising and Title IX was added to the HEA in 1986 to fund programs encouraging black students to pursue graduate study. However, many black institutions have difficulty hiring and retaining faculty, in part because they continue to suffer from unequal funding and are unable to match the salaries offered by white institutions (Henderson 1; Parsons 64). ASU's black women faculty have continued to provide much leadership in pursuing redress of these and other longstanding grievances on campus, establishing an affiliate of the American Federation of Teachers, the Faculty-Staff Alliance, in 1993.

While Great Society legislation helps black institutions in a variety of ways, Title III does not require that they be compensated for state funding inequities, from which they continue to suffer. In 1970, the NAACP filed a complaint, *Adams v. Richardson,* charging the Department of Health, Education and Welfare (HEW) with failure to enforce Title VI of the 1964 Civil Rights Act against states that continued operating segregated systems of public higher education. In 1977, the court ordered HEW to develop guidelines for states to use in preparing desegregation plans, stipulating that black institutions should not be harmed (Roebuck and Murty 40–41). ASU was not a party to this suit, its then president, Levi Watkins, having certified to HUD officials in Washington in 1968 that Alabama was already in compliance with Title VI in order to obtain release of ASU's urban renewal grant funds (Watkins 95). However, in 1981, Watkins organized a similar complaint by ASU alumni, faculty and students—*Knight v. James*—charging Alabama with perpetuating unequal, racially segregated institutions. In 1983, the Department of Justice filed suit against the state of Alabama and its educational institutions, including ASU, alleging that they maintained a racially dual system of public higher education. The court allowed ASU to realign as a plaintiff in this suit (*U.S. v. Alabama*) and, in 1985, allowed the plaintiffs in *Knight v. James* to intervene (Watkins 177–79).

In a series of rulings in the 1990s, federal courts handed defeats to the states but only partial and conditional support to publicly assisted black institutions. While plaintiffs wanted states to fund black institutions on a par with white institutions, courts have instead required states to achieve a higher degree of integration and have placed some of the blame, and burden, on black institutions themselves. In 1991, the U.S. District Court for the Northern District of Alabama found that segregation did persist in higher education in the state of Alabama and the U.S. Supreme Court, ruling the following year on a case from Mississippi, required states to take concrete steps to remove all vestiges of segregation. In the Alabama case, however, the court merely ordered predominantly white institutions to recruit more black faculty—and ordered black institutions to recruit more white students as well. The Justice Department appealed the decision and won a new trial, resulting in a 1995 decision by federal district judge Harold L. Murphy. In the meantime, the Supreme Court's decision in the Mississippi case cast doubt on the legitimacy of supporting both historically black and predominantly white institutions when the two are located next to each other. In keeping with that decision, Murphy ruled that Alabama's two historically black institutions, Alabama State University and Alabama A&M University, "must become institutions not identified solely on the basis of race" (Jaschik A21–A22).

While the 1995 decision caused consternation on campus, it did order valuable new state support for ASU in several areas. The court ordered that ASU be allowed to develop up to two doctoral programs, its first, moving ASU to the highest level of institutional status on a par with the state's premier predominantly white institutions (Healy A28). Today, an EdD program in Educational Leadership, Policy, and Law is in operation and a proposed PhD program in Microbiology has received final approval from the Alabama Council on Higher Education. In addition, the court ordered the state to create a trust fund for academics, the ASU Trust for Educational Excellence, with a goal of reaching at least forty-five million dollars in fifteen years. During this period, the state pays one million dollars a year into the fund and makes a matching contribution of another million dollars each year that ASU, for its part, succeeds in raising at least that amount through its own efforts (Jaschik A21–A22). Finally, the court ordered the state to provide funding for "other race" or "minority" scholarships in order to assist ASU to increase white student enrollment. Today, ASU has largely put behind it heated controversy about these scholarships by raising the GPA required to qualify for them, which it initially had set lower than that for other scholarships (Healy A28).

Conclusion

From The Great Society to No Child Left Behind, our national political agenda has reflected the expanded role that education has come to play in making the new American dream a reality. In the last fifty years, federal support for our educational institutions has grown exponentially and, as a result, far more Americans than ever before pursue higher education and obtain college degrees. The development of the system of higher education that exists in America today is a story in which black Americans and black colleges, including ASU, have played key roles. This story suggests that today's American dream took shape in the historic struggles of black Americans for freedom, most notably in the Civil War and the modern civil rights movement. The Civil War that liberated black Americans from slavery in the South also brought about federal land-grant support that expanded institutions of higher education north and south alike, for whites as well as blacks, while the black struggle for civil rights brought about the federal financial aid programs that bring higher education within the reach of middle-income and lower-income families, white as well as black, throughout the nation.

Seen through the eyes of the twelve academics contributing to this volume, America's more than one hundred historically black colleges and universities have much in common with the many hundreds of predominantly white institutions of higher education in the United States. After all, faculty at Montgomery's black university have the same hopes and aspirations as good university faculty anywhere: to engage their students' interest in intellectual pursuits and inspire them to do their best; to open the doors for them to a broad range of new experiences; to contribute to the sum of human knowledge through research and creative activities within their respective disciplines; and, of course, to receive tangible recognition for their efforts through academic tenure and promotion. Sometimes they drop the ball, just as faculty members sometimes do everywhere.

At the same time, faculty at Montgomery's black university are keenly aware that they are uniquely positioned within the world of higher education. Accounting for just three percent of institutions in the United States, today's HBCUs stand upon a grand tradition, despite the fact that they have always been relatively poor financially. For approximately 214,000 black students and others, they continue to provide a valued alternative to predominantly white institutions (Department of Interior 1). Through the efforts of qualified faculty and others who are called upon to work diligently and patiently, inside and outside the classroom, a great deal continues to be accomplished today. The state-sponsored institutions among them continue to be shortchanged by state legislatures that give funding priority to competing, predominantly white, institutions, despite court findings that such disparities unconstitutionally perpetuate past injustices. As a result, HBCU faculty members teach more on average than do their peers nationwide, and are paid less. They also make do with less in all areas of research and instructional resources, from libraries to offices and classrooms, always playing catch-up with current standards for technology at competing institutions. HBCU faculty members must continually swim upstream—yet most arrive where they need to go, nevertheless.

The community that faculty members describe in this volume is new, but its roots are as old as America itself. Being a part of the continually developing American dream to which they are committed, faculty are aware that their community is a product of the historical developments described in this essay. Aided by their professional academic training, faculty members in ASU's Humanities Department have an especially keen awareness that, without the historical developments described in this essay, their community would not be possible. Certainly, all its members take pride in the role that Montgomery's black university has played, and continues to play, in bringing the American dream within the reach of all Americans. And they are committed to helping to make that dream a reality for any, and all, who enter their classrooms. Indeed, their awareness, pride, and commitment are a few of the hallmarks of this community.

PART ONE

Alabama
Black-White Mix

1 / You Can Go Home Again

Kathy Dunn Jackson

During the 1940s and '50s, Montgomery, Alabama, prided itself on its conservative nature and the fact that it was the so-called Cradle of the Confederacy. Like many southern cities, Montgomery was racially segregated. There were white neighborhoods and black neighborhoods, white schools and black schools, white water fountains, waiting rooms, and restrooms and black water fountains, waiting rooms, and restrooms. Most were clearly marked "white" and "colored." Others were designated simply by tradition.

As a young girl growing up in the city, I knew all about segregation. I really do not recall how I knew—how and when I became aware of this policy. I can only assume it must have been through what I learned at home and at school and through the experiences I had here in the South and in travels to other parts of the country. As I have grown older, I realize that the adults in my childhood allowed me to learn about segregation, but at the same time protected my self-esteem. I felt very secure in my black world and never felt inferior when interacting with whites.

Yet there are some incidents that remain vivid in my memory. One is the time my family witnessed the Ku Klux Klan burning a huge cross atop Stone Mountain as we traveled home one night from visiting my aunt and uncle in Athens, Georgia. I'll also never forget the bombings of Dr. King's and Reverend Abernathy's homes, the latter of which shook our house a block and a half away. And etched in memory is the treatment I received when my tonsils and adenoids were removed the summer of my seventh year.

Because black physicians were not allowed to practice in most of the city hospitals, there were no black ear, nose, and throat specialists in Montgomery and my surgeon was white. I was operated on at St. Margaret's Hospital. After the surgery, I was taken to a small house at the back of the hospital where black patients recuperated. I realized many years later that there was no cover to shield these black patients from the elements as they were transported from the hospital to the house. When I arrived home, my neighborhood friends would visit every day and being the talker that I am, I enjoyed conversing with them. As a result, I awakened one night hemorrhaging because I had broken the stitches. My parents rushed me back to the hospital where I was placed in the house, which contained one large ward where patients lay side by side. I remember some years later my mother saying that a screen was placed around my bed as the nurses tried to stop the hemorrhaging. She recalled that when the doctor arrived, he asked where I was. When the nurse directed him to the bed behind the screen, the doctor said, "Oh, big niggers, huh." I also recall going to the doctor's office downtown for follow-up visits. I remember because it seemed that on each visit we stayed all day. We sat in the "colored" waiting room—the broom closet with a few folding chairs, the broom, mop, bucket, and other cleaning supplies—until all of the white patients had been seen. I was always tired, hungry, and restless. I now can imagine that my mother was seething and that she endured this treatment only because I needed medical attention. However, my mother had her own ways of dealing with racism.

One situation that particularly irked her was the way whites addressed blacks. Regardless of the age of the black person, whites, especially white salespeople, usually referred to the individual by first name. So my mother used initials with the title "Mrs." on her checks and when signing her name. The salespeople were forced to call her Mrs. Dunn or nothing at all. Also when my mother, sister, and I would shop, salesladies, especially at one shop downtown, always referred to the three of us as "girls." My mother was quick to inform them that my sister and I were her "girls" and that she was a fully grown woman and wished to be acknowledged as such. My father also pointed out how whites hated to use "Mr." and "Mrs." for blacks. There was one grocery store where the workers always called him "Prof" or "Dean," both being professional titles which he did hold. However, they never used the title "Mr."—not for him, not for any other black man.

The only places where whites and blacks generally interacted in Montgomery during the 1940s and '50s were on jobs where blacks worked for whites, in businesses that both blacks and whites patronized, and in some neighborhood stores. For instance, in my neighborhood, there were several stores owned by Jewish businessmen. They were patronized for the most part by blacks in the neighborhood; few whites ventured into these stores. However, my neighborhood bordered a white neighborhood near Oak Park. There was one store owned by whites that served both neighborhoods. Sometimes my friends and I would meet white kids at the store, exchange telephone numbers, and call each other from time to time. We knew that we couldn't visit each other, so we didn't even attempt to. We just met at the store and talked on the telephone.

Thus the world in which I grew up in Montgomery was essentially a black world, but it was a happy, secure place and Alabama State College played a great role in its being that way. Recent conversations with those who grew up with me reveal that they too feel that Alabama State provided us with opportunities that we might have otherwise not had.

Alabama State began in 1867 as Lincoln Normal School in Marion, Alabama. This school was financed by the American Missionary Association, the Freedmen's Bureau, the Alabama Legislature, and the colored citizens of Marion. The efforts of Peyton Finley, the first black man to be elected a member of the State Board of Education, to establish a "university for colored people," came to fruition in 1873 when the Alabama Legislature established a "State Normal School and University for the Education of the Colored Teachers and Students." This Act was accompanied by the provision that "the president and trustees of Lincoln Normal School would place that facility at the disposal of the state in order for the new university to be established. The institution's first president, George N. Card, accepted the provision, and in 1874, led the effort to reorganize Lincoln Normal School as America's first state-supported educational institution for blacks" ("History of Alabama State University" 2). After thirteen years in Marion, the school was moved to Montgomery in 1887.

My mother, G. Faustine Hamblin, moved to Montgomery in 1911 when her father, a minister, was assigned to pastor at Old Ship AME Zion Church, the oldest black church in the city. After graduating from Miss White's school in Montgomery, my mother ventured to Livingstone College in Salisbury, North Carolina, where she received her bachelor's degree. She then returned to Montgomery to teach at Alabama State. There, she met and married my father, C. Johnson Dunn, who had been recruited to come to Alabama State by the president, H. Councill Trenholm, one of my father's schoolmates at Morehouse College in Atlanta, Georgia. My parents settled in my mother's home on the edge of the campus, directly across the street from the president's home, in the house purchased by my grandfather before his death. This is where my sister and I grew up, living with our parents and our maternal grandmother. College students lived with us from time to time and helped to care for my sister and me by babysitting and walking us to and from school.

I loved the neighborhood bordering the campus in which I grew up. It had character, unlike many neighborhoods today where the houses and people are all alike. Our home was in the middle of the block and was surrounded by homes owned or rented by people of every economic class and profession. There were many children in my neighborhood, so I always had playmates, and all of the adults in the neighborhood took care of us. We played in each other's yards and if there was a large group, we went to a vacant space on campus such as the side of Kilby Hall to play baseball or to Stewart Hall to swing on the swing sets. During the summer, we went to the movies at least once a week to see the latest serial of Batman or whichever superhero was popular at the time at one of the "colored" theaters, the Pekin, the Art, or the Carver. Our parents gave us dimes for bus fare to avoid the hot sun at matinee time. (At that time people believed that the hot sun contributed to polio, which was epidemic in my childhood.) Once, we decided to walk home and buy ice cream with our bus fare. We waited in the bushes near the bus stop until the bus came and then emerged to go to our different houses. Little did we know that a parent had seen us walking and had alerted the other parents. Not only had we disobeyed by walking in the sun, we also lied about it. Each one of us was spanked. This is how our neighborhood was—the entire village raised us.

The backyard to President Trenholm's home was a block long and the side of it was directly in front of our house. This yard was the setting for all of Alabama State's receptions, many club social activities, and other events. My sister and I enjoyed sitting on our large front porch watching the people come and go, decked in their finery. The president's wife, Mrs. Portia Trenholm, a talented and creative lady, was one of my mother's friends and the Trenholms' youngest child, Harper, was one of my friends, so we often spent time in that big backyard and in the house.

President Trenholm guided Alabama State when there was meager financial support from the state. Yet he found ways to keep the school afloat. Many students arrived on campus without any means of paying for college—just a desire to study. President Trenholm found ways through scholarships and work opportunities to help them pay bills. He made Alabama State one of the best teachers' colleges in the nation. He was also the cornerstone of the American Teachers Association, then the national organization for black teachers, which later merged with the white teachers' organization to become the National Education Association.

I began school at the age of two at Alabama State's nursery/kindergarten under the tutelage of the venerable Miss Wiletta McGinty, who gave hundreds of black kids in Montgomery their first schooling. From the kindergarten in the basement of Beverly Hall, I went across campus to Stewart Hall for grades one through six and then to Old Tullibody for grades seven through twelve. These grades were part of the college's Laboratory School, so called because this is where the college's education majors observed our teachers and practiced their teaching. Today, I often think about the old buildings in which we learned—heated with coal, the soot from which covered everything, windows with no screens, and in Tullibody, bathrooms in the basement which had to be reached by going outside. There were newer, more modern schools for blacks in the city and these schools were free; nevertheless, there remained a waiting list of students trying to enter the Laboratory School. That's because of what went on inside of the school. We had highly trained teachers, most of whom also taught at the college, our classes were small (there was only one section of each class), the rules were strict, the expectations were high, and we had access to the college's facilities, materials, and programs.

The college's reach was broad, affecting not only those who attended school here or those who lived nearby. Alabama State was, in fact, the center of black life in Montgomery. Fortunately, President Trenholm was a man who believed in opportunities for all, so the campus facilities and programs were made available to the public. Black Montgomery came to Tullibody Hall for its culture, to Hornet Stadium for football and baseball games, to the campus center for parties and teas, and to the gymnasium for basketball games, debutante balls, dances, and carnivals.

While sitting in the audience in Tullibody, whether for our weekly Lab High assembly or for a public cultural event, my horizons were broadened.

I heard Marian Anderson and Roland Hayes sing. I reveled in the music of the opera *Carmen*. I sat spellbound at lectures by Charles Wesley, Ralph Bunche, Benjamin Mays, and many other great orators. I witnessed plays, concerts, talent shows, and many other productions by professional and community groups and Alabama State students and staff. At these programs I was exposed to many positive black role models who inspired me to seek to achieve, and who motivated me to dare to dream. While all of my dreams did not come true, the pursuit of them helped to shape my adult life.

The campus also offered a place just to have fun. For instance, every black child in Montgomery wanted a pair of roller skates or a bicycle for Christmas. On Christmas morn and for about a week thereafter, the street in front of Bibb Graves Hall on the Alabama State campus was cordoned off to traffic and every black child tried to make his/her way over to spend the day on "the hill." The young kids would skate and ride bikes up and down the hill all day and the teenagers would meet their friends to "hang out." It was our own private skating rink; it was safe and every parent knew where his/her child was.

On Sunday evenings, my friends and I (all of different religious denominations) walked together to Sunbeam Band (a Baptist activity) at the home of Mrs. Shannon on Hutchinson Street. We actually learned quite a bit about the Bible at this activity. However, our main goal was to walk together to the meeting and then, afterwards, to walk to the Sweet Shoppe on Alabama State's campus for ice cream. If it was not too late when we finished our ice cream (we had to be home before dark), we visited our student teachers and play sisters in the dormitories.

Because my father was athletic director and basketball coach, my friends and I attended all of Alabama State's athletic events. Basketball games were our favorite. In fact, when we were in elementary school, a special box was built in what is now Lockhart Gym for us to sit in at the college games. We even traveled to out-of-town games, especially the SIAC tournament in Tuskegee. At Tuskegee's Logan Gym, all Alabama State fans sat in the east balcony and we watched game after game often until after 1:00 a.m. We dragged to school the next day, but were ready for more games that evening. When I was in junior high, one of the assistant coaches, Doc Crawford, organized a group of us to cheer for the college basketball team. We loved this because we got to be near the basketball players, several of whom we had crushes on. They were always nice and patient with us, but considered us silly preteens, I'm sure. Doc Crawford also taught us to play tennis on the college's tennis courts and Dr. Norman Walton taught us to swim at the college pool. Like many other black students in Montgomery, I also took piano and dance lessons on campus from highly trained instructors. Although I was not talented in any of these areas, all these lessons provided discipline and enjoyment for me and gave me a lifelong appreciation and love of music and dance.

For so many, Alabama State was the center of our lives and because the college offered so much, we did not feel deprived. Of course, there were still those who for one reason or another could not take advantage of what Alabama State had to offer. And there were things that even the school could not provide. Even as kids we knew from news reports and conversations with adults that blacks in the South were denied what was entitled to us as American citizens. Blacks still had to sit in the back of the bus, we were still denied the right to vote and the right to participate in the governance of the city, state, and nation. Black physicians were still denied the right to practice in certain hospitals, and waiting rooms, restrooms, and water fountains were still segregated. Even though new schools were built for blacks, they lacked sufficient libraries and science laboratories, and black students still had to use old, out-dated books.

There was dissatisfaction and unrest, but anyone who dared to challenge the status quo was certain to suffer consequences. As children, my friends and I often heard snatches of whispered conversations among adults about someone losing a job or being forced to leave town because of something that person had said or done that was out of place for a Negro. We had a neighbor who suddenly went to Michigan, leaving his family behind. I never knew what he was supposed to have done, but I heard that he had to leave quickly to avoid trouble. His family joined him a few years later and they never returned here, not even for a visit.

The whispering, the refusal to take a stand, was the cause of much consternation for the Reverend Vernon Johns, who came to Montgomery in 1947 to pastor the Dexter Avenue Baptist Church where my father was a deacon. Reverend Johns often admonished blacks in Montgomery, especially his congregation, most of whom were faculty and administrators at Alabama State, for not taking a stand against discrimination—for not uniting to become more proactive. But people were afraid—many who worked for whites were afraid of losing their jobs when they had families to support. Even the faculty and staff of Alabama State worked at the pleasure of the then all-white State Board of Education. Others were afraid of even greater consequences, perhaps losing their lives—they had seen it happen before. Most people simply endured until they had an opportunity to relocate up north or out west. Many in Reverend Johns's congregation agreed that something needed to be done and quite a few joined his Farmers Enterprise and some of his other projects as a way of gaining economic independence, but overall, his middle-class congregation was embarrassed by him. They were not embarrassed so much by his ideas, but by actions such as selling watermelon from the back of a truck in front of the church and on campus, and wearing overalls and no socks or shoelaces. It was no surprise to many, then, when he and Dexter parted company in 1952. At the time, of course, I did not realize the impact that Reverend Johns had had, but I did miss his wife, who taught piano at Alabama State and his children, with whom my sister and I had become friends. I was happy to run into his daughter Jeanne again when I later took graduate courses at Atlanta University. Fortunately, Reverend Johns had planted some seeds while he was in Montgomery, which were eventually cultivated by other individuals and groups.

One place where seeds were planted was in an organization called the Women's Political Council (WPC), of which my mother was a member. This organization was founded in 1946 by Dr. Mary Fair Burks, chairman of the English Department at Alabama State and a member of Dexter Church. The WPC was formed for the purpose "of inspiring Negroes to live above mediocrity, to elevate their thinking, to fight juvenile and adult delinquency, to register and vote, and in general to improve their status as a group" (Robinson 23). In 1950, Mrs. Jo Ann Gibson Robinson, another English teacher at Alabama State, became president of the WPC. As time progressed, the WPC began to receive complaints from blacks in the city about cases of abuse from whites. Many of these complaints were about the city bus system. Mrs. Robinson and other WPC leaders sought a meeting with the bus company management, at which time the women presented written reports of drivers, bus numbers, hours and routes where incidents had occurred (Robinson 30). The bus company listened to their complaints. Subsequent meetings with bus officials and the city's mayor resulted in a few weeks of better bus service and treatment of black riders. However, the indignities resumed shortly thereafter.

Meanwhile complaints were being heard by other black organizations in the city as well, notably, the Citizens Steering Committee headed by Alabama State employee Mr. Rufus Lewis and the Progressive Democratic Association, headed by Mr. E. D. Nixon. Mr. Nixon, a leader in the Brotherhood of Sleeping Car Porters and the local and state chapters of the NAACP, was often called upon by the black masses in Montgomery who were victims of racial injustice. Another organization, the Interdenominational Ministerial Alliance, composed of ministers of black churches of different faiths in Montgomery, also heard complaints and wanted to take some action.

In 1955, after the arrests and convictions of Claudette Colvin and later Mary Louise Smith, two teenage black girls who refused to give up their seats in the "black" part of the bus to white riders, the black citizenry of Montgomery became more resentful and rebellious. Mrs. Robinson, who had herself experienced great fear and embarrassment when she sat in the front of a bus in 1949, proposed a boycott of the city bus company to the WPC, which took the idea under consideration. According to Mrs. Robinson, the WPC even planned on paper for fifty thousand notices to be distributed calling for a boycott of the buses; "only the specifics of time and place had to be added" (Robinson 39). But there were doubters who wanted to be sure that the women had the support of most of the blacks in the city. Others were concerned that the teenagers were too young to be the center of the boycott. The arrest of Mrs. Rosa Parks on December 1, 1955, a story known throughout the world, was the catalyst needed to gel the organizations of black Montgomery and channel the resentment and rebelliousness of the people into action in the form of a bus boycott.

Like everyone else, my family and I participated in the boycott. We attended mass meetings, we walked, and my father often transported others in his car. Living across the street from one bus stop and three houses away from another, my mother, sister, and I had always ridden the bus to town to shop and my friends and I had taken the bus to our other activities. During the boycott, even though our parents carpooled to take us places, transportation was not always available, and because of the dangers of being out, especially at night, we had to give up some of our normal teenage activities. As everyone knows, learning to drive is uppermost in most teenagers' minds and many of us were approaching the age when we could get a learner's permit. However, because blacks were often stopped by the police during the boycott and falsely accused of violations, our parents did not want us to drive. To compensate for the activities we lost during the boycott, Mrs. Hazel

James, a secretary at Alabama State and the mother of one of my friends, gathered together several parents, including my mother, in 1955 to charter a chapter of Jack and Jill of America, Inc., in Montgomery. This organization, which was begun in Philadelphia, Pennsylvania, emphasized families working together to provide wholesome activities for their own children and others in the community. Jack and Jill was a bright light in my life at that time as our families banded together to provide cultural and social activities that would have been difficult for an individual family to provide during these trying times. Jack and Jill remains one of my favorite organizations today.

During the boycott, the seeds that Reverend Johns had planted earlier at Dexter Church came to full fruition under the leadership of Dr. Martin Luther King Jr. This young, articulate minister had the same great intelligence and courage of Reverend Johns, but in a more conservative way, and so his parishioners and other blacks in the city were more willing to follow his lead. Many of his parishioners were Alabama State employees, including President Trenholm.

In general, people from Alabama State served in great numbers as leaders and workers in the bus boycott. But what was the official stance of the college? Certainly, President Trenholm knew that the involvement of the college would be detrimental to the institution, himself, the faculty, staff, and students—that involvement might even close the doors of the school—so he participated and encouraged others connected to the school to do so behind the scenes and to continue being diligent in their work on campus. He and his wife secretly contributed money, advice, and guidance.

As all of the world knows, the bus boycott was a success. After a year of black people walking, carpooling, and sacrificing, the Supreme Court ruled that the city buses could not segregate or discriminate. Although few if any whites rode the bus into our all-black neighborhood, it was a thrilling victory for us to be able to board even an empty bus and sit wherever we wanted or just to watch other blacks do the same. After all, we paid the same fare as any other rider. Most of my schoolmates who rode the bus to and from school immediately made use of this new privilege.

Following the boycott, blacks in Montgomery realized the importance of voting, so efforts were stepped up to register people to vote. These efforts were led by Mr. Rufus A. Lewis, a coach at Alabama State and owner of the Citizens Club, a popular local nightspot. It is said that in order to enter the club, one had to show that s/he was a registered voter. To do our part, several of my friends and I went house to house in our neighborhoods during the summer distributing literature encouraging people to register to vote, and we ourselves registered as soon as we became old enough.

In the fall of 1958, I left Montgomery to attend Fisk University in Nashville, Tennessee. I knew that I would miss my family and friends, but I was excited about going away. Little did I realize that I was exchanging the "frying pan" for the "boiling pot," for during my sophomore year, the student sit-ins and marches began in Nashville. Diane Nash, one of the leaders of the Nashville sit-in movement, lived in the same dormitory that I did, so bomb threats became a common occurrence for us. We often would have to clear the dorm two or three times a night. Most of my schoolmates and I participated in the marches down Jefferson Street to the downtown area. When I came home for spring break that year, along with others from Montgomery, Selma, and Tuskegee, we were met at the train station by our families and several white men in dark suits who followed us to our cars and then to our homes. As my father turned into our driveway, the men following our car kept going. Upon inquiry, my father learned that the men were law enforcement officers who had been notified by the trainmaster in Nashville that a group of students had purchased tickets for Montgomery and were scheduled to arrive at 10:30 that night. He thought that we might be coming to demonstrate. Upon learning that we had come to visit our families during spring break, the officers left us alone.

Meanwhile the student sit-in movement also spread to Montgomery and "on February 25, 1960, Alabama State College students staged their first sit-in demonstration at the snack bar of the Montgomery County Court House. On the following day, Governor John Patterson ordered them expelled and threatened to cut off state funds to the school if the protest continued" (Seay 220). Other students marched to the campus and threatened to boycott classes. The governor fired Dr. Lawrence Reddick, a history teacher who was one of the faculty leaders of the protest, a member of the Dexter Church, and one of Dr. King's close friends.

The next major civil rights movement for Montgomery came in May 1961 when the Freedom Riders arrived in the city. The Freedom Riders, a racially integrated group organized by the Congress of Racial Equality to test accommodations in interstate travel, began in Washington, D.C., and traveled south. It encountered violence in Gadsden and Birmingham, Alabama, and its members were promised protection from Birmingham to Montgomery. Upon arrival in Montgomery, they were met by a vicious mob who beat the Riders mercilessly. Montgomery was definitely not ready to roll out the welcome mat. The following Sunday night, a mass meeting led by Dr. Martin L. King Jr. and Reverend Ralph Abernathy was held at the black First Baptist Church. A white mob surrounded the church and law-enforcement officers surrounded the mob. Those inside were forced to stay all night. When daylight dawned, the mob began to disperse and the mass meeting finally ended.

As the civil rights movement moved from the boycott to sit-ins and marches (led primarily by college students around the nation) to the Freedom Riders, Alabama State College's involvement became more disturbing to the white power structure. There were those who believed that faculty at Alabama State were encouraging more student participation, and some teachers were investigated by a special state committee. Political pressures on the college increased. Some professors were dismissed; others resigned under pressure or because conditions had changed. Among those who resigned were Mrs. Robinson and Dr. Mary Fair Burks, the organizer of the WPC. According to Mrs. Robinson, the mental strain they suffered as a result of the boycott, the sit-ins, and harassment from the state's education department took its toll. They were simply weary. Each resigned without knowing that the others were planning to leave. They left with regret but also with the understanding, blessings, and friendship of President Trenholm, and they remained friends with the Trenholm family. While there were those who left Alabama State, there were just as many or more who remained. Among them were my parents, Mr. and Mrs. J. E. Pierce, Mr. and Mrs. Arthur Glass, Mr. John Cannon, Mr. and Mrs. F. W. Taylor, Mrs. Olean Underwood, and Mr. Rufus Lewis. Many had families, so pulling up stakes might have been more difficult for them. Or they simply may have decided that they would not be run off from their jobs and homes. Whatever the reasons, many stayed until they retired years later.

In the meantime, the State Board of Education decided that President Trenholm had lost control of the faculty and students. The power of the presidency was taken away from him although he remained in office. This great man, who had given his all to the school, the faculty and staff, and the students for thirty-six years, became broken in spirit and body. Not long after, he became too ill to work, and was forced to retire on January 1, 1962. He died about a year later. We all lost a good friend and great role model.

After graduating from Fisk in the spring of 1962, I moved to Ann Arbor, Michigan, for graduate school at the University of Michigan. As was the custom at that time, my graduate studies were compensated in part by the state of Alabama to keep me from trying to attend graduate school at one of the universities here. I spent part of my time in graduate school teaching high school English in Toledo, Ohio. Upon receiving my master's degree, I had several job offers, all from colleges in the South. A winter in Maine on exchange from Fisk and two winters in Michigan and Ohio convinced me that I am a warm-weather person. I decided to accept the offer that I had received to teach at Alabama State, so that I could live at home, save money, and buy a car. Waiting for a bus in the snow had been no fun. So, I returned to Alabama State to teach during the 1964–65 school year.

By this time, the national civil rights movement was escalating. People from all over the world were participating and black Montgomerians, emboldened by the success of the bus boycott, were in the midst of it all. During the 1965 Selma-to-Montgomery march, Alabama State faculty, staff, and students were marching out of classes to participate. My father said that if people from around the world were willing to fight for our rights, we had to do our part, too. We housed a college student from New York who had come to march. My office mate, Ernestine Slade, who was another young English teacher, and I joined the march at St. Jude and made our way to the State Capitol with all of the others.

Slowly, but surely, Montgomery's staunch segregationist policies were crumbling. The Supreme Court decision of 1956 enabled blacks to sit in any seats on the city buses. The Freedom Rides opened accommodations in interstate travel. Public eating places were opened to blacks as a result of the sit-in movement and the march from Selma to Montgomery brought voting rights. Public parks in Montgomery were desegregated several years after a case was filed in 1958 on behalf of a teenager, Mark Gilmore, who was arrested for walking through Oak Park to get to his job at Jackson Hospital. The city closed the parks the next year rather than integrate them. When Judge Frank Johnson ruled that parks must be integrated if they were ever reopened, they remained closed for about six years. When the parks finally reopened, the swimming pool in the city's largest park, Oak Park, became a duck pond. As my children played in Oak Park years later, I often thought of how I was denied that privilege when I was a child. In spite of strides in other areas, Montgomery's public schools were still segregated ten years after the 1954 *Brown v. Board of Education* decision. In April of 1964, a lawsuit was filed on behalf of Arlam Carr Jr. and others to desegregate the public schools of the city. Judge Frank Johnson issued a ruling that the schools were to begin integration in the fall of 1964. My next-door neighbor, Patricia Oliver, was among the first to attend Sidney Lanier High School, the city's elite white high school. Although there were some hecklers and picketers, the integration of the school was fairly smooth. In 1965, black physicians, previously denied staff privileges at the city's white hospitals, were admitted to memberships on the staffs at St. Margaret's and Jackson Hospitals.

Meanwhile, Alabama State, which had been founded as an institution for educating blacks and which had operated that way throughout the years, made an effort to recruit white students. The school hired three white student admissions officers and offered tuition with renewal to white students if they maintained a "B" average (Watkins 159). The tactic had little success.

Then, in 1969, Auburn University established a branch in Montgomery (AUM) on the opposite side of town from Alabama State. Like most Alabama State supporters, I was disturbed by the establishment of another state college in Montgomery, because it would divide financial support from the state. Eventually, however, AUM became an asset to me. In the early 1970s, I began taking doctoral courses at Auburn's main campus. Thereafter, I was able to take courses at AUM during evening hours as I continued to teach at Alabama State during the day. I took courses on the main campus on weekends and during the summer. By continuing to teach full-time, I was able to help keep our family income at the same level and to accumulate years in the retirement system, allowing me to retire early.

The first white professors in my department, at that time the English department, came to Alabama State in the late 1960s and early '70s. They were two white females of southern origin, well educated and well traveled. The two, Martha Biggs and June Zimmerman, became not only my colleagues but also my good friends. Both remained at Alabama State until they retired in the 1990s. Through the years, other whites joined the general faculty as well as our departmental faculty, and as chair of the Humanities department for twelve years (1986–98), I hired many whites.

I actually do not recall my first white student at Alabama State. I do know that through the 1970s and '80s, there would be a white student in one of my classes on occasion. In 1995, when the District Court ruled that historically black colleges in Alabama should receive increases in funding from the state to attract minority students, more whites began to come. For the first time, I sometimes had more white students in some of my classes than black. By then, most students had attended integrated elementary and high schools, so black and white students were accustomed to being together. I think that both groups of students sometimes approached a required course that I taught, Humanities through the African American Experience, with a little apprehension when the class was mixed. However, although the course did include some race-sensitive content, the intent was not to make anyone feel ill at ease. After the class began, students started to feel comfortable with the material, with each other and with me. We always made use of Montgomery's history with segregation and civil rights by visiting historic sites and conducting interviews with people who had personal experience in both movements, and by the end of the semester, students usually expressed appreciation for such an enlightening course.

Today, Montgomery is very different from the city in which I grew up. Neighborhoods, businesses, and schools are now integrated. Many blacks who grew up here but moved north in search of a better racial climate have felt able to return here to retire because of the changes that have taken place. My children's experiences growing up in Montgomery were very different from mine. Although they attended Alabama State's Early Childhood Center through kindergarten, they went to integrated public schools during their elementary and high school years. The college's Laboratory School, which I attended, was closed in 1971. Whereas Alabama State was the center of my educational, cultural and social life, my children's activities extended all over the city in integrated theaters, parks, skating rinks, and other venues.

Alabama State is a very different place, too. The small college where I grew up with everyone as part of a family no longer exists. When I was young, people came to work at Alabama State and stayed, if not for a lifetime, at least for a number of years. Today, the employees are more mobile; they come one year and often move on the next. The workforce is now large, diverse, and divided—people often do not know each other unless they work in the same department. The college has been a university since 1969, and the campus has grown tremendously.

The relationship between the college and the state and city has changed.

Alabama State has its own Board of Trustees now. State and city governments, which in the past usually ignored the school unless there was some disturbance concerning racial issues, are now more involved, especially in financial support. Black legislators and senators, many of whom are graduates of Alabama State and/or who work there, make sure that the school is included in their proceedings.

While growing up on the campus of Alabama State in Montgomery, I never thought that I would return here to spend most of my adulthood. I always imagined spending that part of my life elsewhere. And once I left these environs, I felt as George Webber did in Thomas Wolfe's novel, that you can't go home again, at least not to live. But my life's path eventually led back to Montgomery and to Alabama State. Home, as they say, is where the heart is, and ultimately, I found my heart here. I taught on a campus I loved, surrounded by people I love, married an Alabama State graduate I loved, and settled into life "at home."

2 / E Pluribus Unum

Discovering Multiculturalism

Virginia M. Jones

The lands around my dwelling
Are more beautiful
From the day
When it is given to me to see
Faces I have never seen before.
All is more beautiful.
All is more beautiful.
And life is thankfulness.
These guests of mine
Make my home grand.
                    —Eskimo Prayer

I was raised in the South, but I did not know the South. I lived most of my childhood and adolescence in Birmingham, but one day in 1963 I discovered that I did not know Birmingham. My family and I were watching the evening news when the television screen was filled with pictures of boys and girls being attacked by snarling German shepherds and battered by high-powered streams of water pouring from fire hoses. Meanwhile, I heard the most shocking words I could remember: "In Birmingham, Alabama, today . . ." Who were these people, faces twisted grotesquely by anger and hatred, attacking teenagers and children? Who were these bleeding black children? Where did they come from? What did they do that so infuriated the white people? I did not know, but I was determined to answer my questions.

Almost all my life, I had seen signs that read "white" or "colored," but I was totally unaware of the reality reflected by them. When I first could read the word "colored" over a water fountain, I thought it contained rainbow-colored water. Although I saw "colored" people on the streets, in the stores, and on the buses, I did not know them. African Americans did not live in my neighborhood, attend my school, or worship in my church.

Until I graduated from high school in 1964, I only knew two African Americans. One was a very friendly, elderly man who worked in my grandmother's yard in Summit, Mississippi. Everyone called him Uncle Jim; and, when I was a small child, I thought he was one of my uncles. The other African American was a very kind young woman named Catherine, who took care of my sisters and me when my mother was very ill after the birth of my youngest sister. To me, Catherine was family too. In 1963, when I watched the horrible treatment of Birmingham's black children during the Children's March, I wanted to meet more African Americans and to discover more about the reasons for the march, but how? So, I began a journey that in 1981 led me to Alabama State University, where I found many answers.

The first stage of my journey was an emotional and intellectual roller coaster. Since I could not seek information from African Americans directly, I was forced to rely on secondary sources, mainly television reports, newspaper articles, and books. My intellectual curiosity was converted into a passionate desire for change during the summer when I watched the television coverage of the March on Washington and listened to Dr. King's speech. Obviously, many Americans were treated unjustly, especially in the South. I glimpsed the depth and extent of the hatred and fear that fueled these injustices in the fall of 1963; four young girls in Birmingham died when their church was bombed during Sunday School. Soon after the deadly church bombing, President Kennedy was assassinated. The hopeful innocence of my youth ended; I was sixteen.

Suddenly, violent activities seemed to generate even more violence. Frequently, in my South even nonviolent activities were countered with violent responses. Freedom Riders, sit-in participants, black and white marchers were cursed, beaten, threatened, and even killed. Dr. King was jailed in Birmingham, but the church bombers were not arrested. When my family traveled to Boston to visit my mother's family in the summer of 1964, I was ashamed of the Alabama license tags on our car. I loved being a southerner, but I was beginning to hate the South.

In a frustrating attempt to make sense out of this chaotic world in which I lived, I read every book I could find written by or about African Americans, but finding such books was difficult. One of my first discoveries was *To Kill a Mockingbird*. Atticus Finch was an accurate picture of the white southerners I knew. Some of the other books I read but did not truly understand were *Native Son, Invisible Man, Go Tell It on the Mountain,* and *A Raisin in the Sun.* Almost forty years later, I'm still learning what they mean.

In August 1964 I entered the Benedictine Convent in Cullman, Alabama. Many of the nuns were actively involved in the civil rights movement; for example, some marched from Selma to Montgomery to support voting rights. I was a novice and was not permitted to leave the convent grounds during that year. Nevertheless, I did as much as I could to participate in the struggle for equal rights. As more and more Catholic churches and schools were integrated, the nuns became magnets for the hopes and fears of southern Catholics; we tried to be leaders for justice, but often became victims of hatred ourselves. I was cursed and even spat upon, but I was on a quest to create a better community that accepted, even welcomed all citizens. In 1968 Dr. King was assassinated; Bobby Kennedy was killed; the Vietnam War escalated; death was everywhere. My quest seemed an impossible dream for, as the popular song went, no one seemed to like anyone very much.

The next year, I took a giant leap forward on my unknown journey towards Alabama State. I was assigned to teach freshman religion at the newly integrated Pensacola Catholic High School. In the previous year, the faculty and students of the small black Catholic high school had been combined with the larger white Catholic school, so I had my first opportunity to teach at a truly integrated school. However, the road to integration was a rocky one. The African American students were distressed that their school had been closed and they were forced to transfer to another school, in which they became a minority of twenty percent of the student body. The white students were resentful that they were required to attend school with African Americans. Because of the fears and resentments, the white students stayed together in the classrooms, the lunchroom, and the gymnasium; likewise, the black students stayed with their friends. During the two years I was at Catholic High, I witnessed a slow transition from separate groups to the beginnings of a community.

Eventually, the barriers eroded, and gradually black and white students became acquaintances and sometimes even friends. I benefited greatly from this process because I also was transformed from an outside observer and avid student of African American culture to a part of this new, partially integrated community.

I was not intimately involved in such a community again until I became a graduate teaching assistant at Georgia State University in Atlanta in 1976, after I left the convent. Almost ten years had passed; integration was commonplace; the segregation laws had been abolished. Legally—but not psychologically, socially, or spiritually—the South had changed.

At Georgia State at least one-third of each of my classes was African American. Through class discussions and, more importantly, through reading essays and counseling with individual students, I was introduced to the social customs, beliefs, values, hopes, and fears of a wide diversity of students. The more I learned about various cultures, the more I wanted to know. Therefore, during the final stage of writing my doctoral dissertation, I applied to join the Peace Corps.

For many years after I had left the convent, I wanted to work as a Peace Corps volunteer in an African nation. My cousin had spent a year as a student missionary in Zimbabwe as part of his seminary training to become a Methodist minister. His year in Africa radically changed my Mississippi cousin; I wanted to experience such a transformation. I knew that as a Peace Corps volunteer I would probably gain much more than I contributed. Unfortunately, the only openings available the year I applied were in Thailand. At that time, my interest in Asian cultures was small, so I decided to wait a year to see if a position in Africa became available. I had just made this decision when I saw an advertisement for a position as an assistant professor of English and Humanities at Alabama State University. I applied, interviewed, and was offered the position within six weeks. The changes I sought in Africa would occur in Montgomery, Alabama.

I joined the faculty in August 1981, two weeks after I was awarded my doctoral degree in American literature. Since I had never worked in the same place for more than three years, I thought I would teach at ASU for a short time and then join the Peace Corps when a desirable position was available. Twenty years later, I'm still in Montgomery. The city and the university are the ideal places for me to explore my questions about the South and diverse cultures. The journey I began in Birmingham in 1963 led to a historically black university.

When I became a part of Alabama State, I suddenly became a minority. Ironically, the first two people I met on campus were white. When I came for my interview, I was greeted by Michael Howley, a New Yorker who had been an instructor at St. Bernard College, less than three miles from Sacred Heart Convent where I had been a Benedictine nun. He introduced me to Dr. Robert Polk Thompson, the dean of University College. The first African American I met was Dr. T. Clifford Bibb, the third person who was present for my interview. Six weeks later, I met the chair of the Humanities Department, Dr. Alma Freeman. Soon, Dr. Freeman replaced Dr. Thompson as dean of University College, and another gifted professional woman, Dr. Kathy Dunn Jackson, became department chair. Dr. Freeman and Dr. Jackson created a college and a department that were more like a family than many natural birth families. They challenged me, encouraged me, and supported me in every way. In fact, when both my parents became seriously ill simultaneously, I was granted a leave of absence to care for them in Atlanta. At the end of that year, I planned to resign because my parents were still too ill to leave and I thought I could not receive another leave of absence. Dr. Roosevelt Steptoe would not accept my letter of resignation; instead, he granted me an unprecedented second year. At the end of that year, my mother came to live with me in Montgomery. As her health deteriorated, Dr. Jackson kindly adapted my teaching schedule so that I could care for my mother. Without the generous support and kind consideration of Dr. Jackson, Dr. Freeman, and the other department faculty, I could not have coped with my mother's deteriorating condition and eventual death in 1992. Although I am a minority at Alabama State, I have never felt like an outsider.

After I had been teaching at State for two quarters, I realized something significant; I did not think about my students as African Americans. They were simply and profoundly only college students. They were intelligent, curious, creative, motivated young people who were often making great sacrifices to attend school in order to increase their opportunities for success. Even though I was a white instructor, I was always treated by the students with respect, acceptance, and oftentimes even affection. In the twenty years I have taught here, I have never experienced the anger, fear, rejection, or hatred that majorities too often inflict on minorities.

Perhaps the main reasons I was hired were that the department needed a humanities instructor and I had a strong educational background in theology and philosophy to accompany my degrees in literature. In the '80s the students were required to take Humanities 101 and Humanities 102. These courses used the textbook *The Humanities: A Cross-Cultural Approach,* written by two of the faculty, Dr. T. Clifford Bibb and Robert Ely. This textbook explored the themes of heroism, imprisonment, rebellion, and freedom in

Western, Eastern, and African cultures. I was familiar with the histories, philosophies, literature, art, and music of Western cultures, but I knew little about these areas in African and Asian cultures. Consequently, I spent many hours researching these unknown areas and discussing various aspects of them with my colleagues. During the first years I taught humanities, I'm sure I learned much more than my students learned.

Thus, I grew in many ways. For example, my mother had instilled in me a love for the blues; however, now I was researching and enjoying many other types of African American music, such as gospel, Dixieland, jazz, and even early rap music. The richness, diversity, and complexity of these musical forms were astonishing and delightful. Also, I became fascinated with the many forms of West African art, particularly its many parallels with Native American art. In addition, I explored aspects of Eastern art, especially the contrasts between Indian and Chinese artistic styles. Instead of simply learning about African American culture, I was now studying world cultures.

Perhaps the most interesting part of teaching these humanities courses for me was that students were required to produce an original artwork in literature, music, art, or dance. Although some students spent little time on their creative projects, many students painted, drew, and sculpted extraordinary works. The musicians composed and performed jazz, blues, and gospel songs. The dancers interpreted traditional African dances or choreographed dance interpretations of classical works or lengthy poems, such as James Weldon Johnson's "Creation" poem from the collection *God's Trombones*. The writers delighted their fellow students with poetry, short stories, myths, and legends. In fact, I was so impressed by the talents of my students that I wanted to share their best works with a wider audience. My colleagues who were teaching humanities agreed, so we held a humanities festival each spring. Students' sculptures, drawings, and paintings were displayed; a booklet containing poems and stories was distributed; an hour-long variety show was organized and presented in the auditorium. Although we no longer have a yearly humanities festival, we still publish the best student essays, research papers, poetry, interviews, and stories in a collection called *Lifted Voices*. The concerns and interests of the students often reflect the concerns of artists, writers, and musicians of the past.

After several years, a new core curriculum class, Humanities 103: Humanities through the African American Experience, replaced the requirement to take Humanities 101 and 102. Many students, however, continued to take these classes. Unfortunately, the textbook we had been using was no longer published, so we were forced to use a book that traced the development of American culture by focusing primarily on the history and achievements of European cultures. My dissatisfaction with this traditional approach motivated me to write a new, multicultural textbook. In order to pursue this project, I needed to educate myself further regarding Eastern cultures. I was invited to participate in an institute on Indian and southeast Asian cultures at the East-West Center in Honolulu, Hawaii, in the summer of 1994. Three years later, I attended an institute on Japanese culture at San Diego State University. In 1999, Alabama State University was chosen by the Japan Foundation to be one of two sites in the country to host a six-week program called the Japan Studies Faculty Development Institute. I was both a presenter and one of the twenty participants in this program designed to aid faculty in introducing Asian cultures into their courses. While filling the gaps in my own education regarding world cultures, I realized that all these societies were represented in the United States. Therefore, I decided my new humanities textbook would simply explore the diverse cultures of America.

This textbook, *We, the People,* is based on the belief that diversity can be one of America's greatest assets. At times, however, multiculturalism has been a tragic liability. The challenge facing Americans and all people in "the global village" is to understand that diversity enriches human life. People travel many roads to the same destinations. I have gradually formulated two fundamental ideas while I have been at Alabama State University, and they are the foundation of the humanities courses I teach and of the textbook I have been writing. The ideas are simple. People in all times and in all places are alike in many ways. Also, people in all times and in all places are different, but different does not mean that one person is right and the other is wrong, one is good and the other is bad, one is superior and the other is inferior. If Americans could allow people to look, to think, and to act differently and not make judgments about their appearance, ideas, or behaviors, then many political, social, economic, and personal problems would disappear. Once people respect the differences among various cultures, they can more fully understand and appreciate their own values, traditions, beliefs, and ethical systems. Any multicultural study finally reveals that people from all times and in all places are much more alike than they are different. As Maya Angelou states in one of her poems, "Human Family":

In minor ways we differ.
In major we're the same. (125)

Each person is free to accentuate his similarities with all people or to focus on her differences from others. Multicultural studies examine, respect, and affirm the value of both the similarities and differences within the human family.

I am privileged to work at Alabama State University in Montgomery, Alabama. My intellectual curiosity about African Americans and my outrage at the injustices they experienced in Alabama have been transformed into a passionate belief in the value of multiculturalism and diversity. Dr. King once said, "Injustice anywhere is a threat to justice everywhere." Learning about the artistic creations, histories, triumphs, and sufferings of African Americans, Asian Americans, Hispanic Americans, Arabic Americans, and Native Americans has not diminished me or threatened my identity as a European American. Instead, I have grown intellectually, morally, and spiritually. I will continue to learn about the cultures of all the people of our nation. I celebrate all the people who live in the United States. Out of many people has been created one nation; and, indeed, Langston Hughes was right. Every person from these diverse cultures is beautiful, and together we are America.

3 / Genesis of the National Center for the Study of Civil Rights and African-American Culture

Janice R. Franklin

Martin L. King Jr., in his *Address to the First Montgomery Improvement Association (MIA) Mass Meeting*, delivered at Montgomery's Holt Street Baptist Church on December 5, 1955, following the arrest of Mrs. Rosa Parks, said, "Right here in Montgomery, when the history books are written in the future, somebody will have to say, 'There lived a race of people, a black people, fleecy locks and black complexion,' a people who had the moral courage to stand up for their rights. And thereby they injected a new meaning into the veins of history and of civilization" (King *Autobiography* 61). Where had I heard this phrase, "fleecy locks and black complexion," I wondered while reading this famous speech. Somewhere deep within, I remembered these words and their powerful, transforming, and inspiring meaning. The phrase surfaced from the recesses of my mind as I suddenly recalled William Cowper's poem "The Negro's Complaint," written in 1788 as a lament on slavery:

Fleecy locks and black complexion
Cannot forfeit Nature's claim;
Skins may differ, but affection
Dwells in black and white the same.

As if it were a nursery rhyme, I heard these words ring in my ear each time my mother recited them during my childhood. These empowering phrases rang out in family conversations as my parents encouraged us to excel in all of our pursuits, regardless of the color of our skin. After much reflection, I clearly understood the reason that I had been driven to work for the advancement of a center for the study of civil rights and African American culture at a place most worthy—the historic campus of Alabama State University.

Because of their fleecy locks and black complexions, the students and faculty of Alabama State University were faced with discrimination that compelled them to join hands with the black community in Montgomery in an act of nonviolent protest for civil rights. With moral courage, they sacrificed their lives to stand up for justice during Montgomery's infamous bus boycott, student sit-ins, and voting rights period of our history. It is a valiant story that should be chronicled in all historical accounts of these events in American history.

For this reason, the quest to establish a center for repository and research that will embrace our history has become my own life's mission while working as library director at Alabama State University. With passion, I work today to ensure that the stories of our civil rights heritage can be preserved, particularly those recording the role of Alabama State University, whose rich history as an early center for teacher education and as the intellectual hub for the modern civil rights movement is not widely known. Out of this historical and personal context, I accepted the calling to lead a project creating a center for the study of civil rights and African American culture.

In August 1997 Dr. William H. Harris, then president of Alabama State University, convened a committee of staff, faculty, and administrators to plan such a center at Alabama State University, where much of the movement was conceived, and to determine the feasibility of building its endowment with the support of the National Endowment for the Humanities' prestigious Challenge Grant. The committee was united in its purpose to formalize the disparate historical library collections, people, activities, events, and multimedia materials on civil rights and African American culture that were available at ASU under the auspices of a center for research.

This charge led to the university's official designation of the National Center for the Study of Civil Rights and African-American Culture at Alabama State University and, in the year 2000, a $500,000 Challenge Grant from the National Endowment from the Humanities to build a two million dollar endowment. ASU was one of only seven institutions that received this award in that year, and the grant review team at NEH was especially impressed with the urgency of the project, the importance of the existing collection, the critical need for preservation, and the plans for becoming a clearinghouse for cultural tourism. In the words of NEH Challenge Grant officials, our university was viewed as an ideal location for a national center that would help preserve a vital part of our American heritage.

At the initial meeting in 1997, I was asked to serve as project director in order to plan and coordinate this historic effort together with outstanding members of the ASU faculty, staff, and administration who formed the steering committee. Out of the original group, a team of dedicated individuals emerged who worked tirelessly to plan the mission and build the endowment for the National Center. The fundraising efforts would later include a $300,000 legislative appropriation for the project's operations from State Representative John Knight, an alumnus of the University and Steering Committee member. The twofold mission became: to serve as a clearinghouse for information concerning the pivotal role of Montgomery, Alabama, in the shaping and development of the modern civil rights movement; and to preserve and disseminate information reflective of socioeconomic conditions, political culture, and history of African Americans in Montgomery.

Although the focus was on Montgomery, the steering committee envisioned a larger national scope that would allow visitors at a distance access to the National Center via its Internet Web site that connected on-site digitized resources to those beyond our own walls. Extending our archives across the curriculum of the university and throughout the world has positioned our Center to be an essential resource for preserving the historic civil rights legacy in Montgomery, and particularly at ASU. Among the many little known historical facts to be disseminated worldwide are the following:

- Many of the emancipation proclamation programs in Montgomery, dating back to the 1800s, were held at the State Normal campus now known as Alabama State University, making it significant in Reconstruction-era history in Alabama.
- ASU's legacy of protest and resistance to injustice has spanned the periods of the bus boycott, the early student sit-in movement, and the voting rights march from Selma to Montgomery.

• Prestigious historians and eminent scholars such as Dr. John Hope Franklin taught at ASU, providing exceptional learning opportunities to students, many of whom assumed teaching responsibilities around the country.

• ASU students and faculty were on the front lines in the Montgomery bus boycott.

• ASU students were expelled for their involvement in the demonstrations and faculty lost their jobs because they participated in the struggle for civil rights in Montgomery.

• The Women's Political Council worked often behind the scenes to lay the groundwork for the protest movement.

• Jo Ann Robinson, an ASU professor and president of the Women's Political Council, sacrificed her university job by duplicating flyers announcing the bus boycott on ASU's campus after the arrest of Mrs. Rosa Parks.

These facts entitle ASU to recognition for its rich history and role in sparking the modern civil rights movement in America. For too long, the university has paid the price for assuming this role as the intellectual center for the movement and for black education. It has fought for its existence after having been originally established in Marion, Alabama, by former slaves who sought the assistance of the American Missionary Association, known after the *Amistad* event for sending teachers from northern cities to educate Negroes in the South. A racial incident in Marion led to its relocation to Montgomery, thereby ensuring—seemingly by divine intervention— its strategic location in history for future civil rights activities. Although the school's relocation was later followed by its designation as a state institution, ASU would face persecution from the government of Alabama, which controlled its management and allocated inequitable funding for the school. Intervention into the administration of the school by state officials resulted in the firing of employees, dismissal of students, and the loss of dignity and respect as the school's progress was stifled because of its involvement in the great movement. ASU's own administration was unjustly forced to participate in firings and dismissals in an attempt to bring order to the school. Yes, ASU has a rightful place in the annuals of history that must be recorded, taught, protected, and honored for its early sacrifices that led to human rights victories around the world.

With this mission to right the wrongs, the National Center has an urgency to establish its national focus. Although it has been born out of a recent initiative, it continues the legacy at ASU to inform students of their heritage as they matriculate within its walls. The National Center's focus as a place for researching civil rights and African American culture is not considered to be a new vision, but instead, part of a continuum of events. ASU, like many other historically black colleges and universities, has stored memorabilia and offered classes in Negro history from its very beginnings to keep alive the truth of our history.

African Americans owe much to our institutions of higher learning. They are the last strongholds of our community, symbols of our progress out of slavery. These institutions preserved our history the best they could. Without the luxury of sophisticated methodologies for preserving historical documents, our institutions, in spite of these challenges, were able to hold onto rare papers, artifacts, precious artworks and books housed in libraries often without full knowledge of their later value. The work of early black leaders, teachers, students, and scholars, who could not attend white universities or be employed there, was kept alive within our own institutions. These documents lay extant with little interest in their value from the majority society, who at that time envisioned no rewards or commercial success from embracing black history. With the black pride movement of the '60s, symbols and records of our history increased in value. Prior to this period, our own people had often been "mis-educated," as described by Carter G. Woodson, by beliefs instilled from white society that Negro history was of little worth. But for the dedication of early educators in historically black colleges and universities, including very determined librarians who knew differently, this history, so precious today, would have been lost. Great treasures still remain undisturbed in many historically black colleges and universities. Perhaps left in boxes on untended shelves, or even within the great minds of its scholars who sacrificed to teach, the collections at our institutions were maintained by those who understood their significance long before centers or museums were established to house and treasure them.

A new paradigm for understanding the value of our history, particularly the commercial value, is needed today. The recent "appreciation" and competition for its ownership among other cultures may not be all bad if it spurs African Americans to reevaluate our role in protecting our own culture. After all, this new climate of competition for our heritage may alert us to the need to support our institutions and not delegate to others the responsibility of being caretakers of the history that we should hold dear. This may, indeed, be a wake-up call to realize the beauty of our culture, its value today in light of its uniqueness, and the importance of our institutions in providing a forum for telling our stories our own way. The gold rush for the right to own this cultural heritage should remind us of the importance of preserving our institutions just as they have preserved our history during the early years of struggle.

Our work in the National Center at ASU is one of service to this cause. We at ASU will accomplish our mission and vision through the preservation of many prestigious collections that are currently housed in our university archives and through the amassing of future collections valuable to establishing the truth of what happened both at our university and in Montgomery. It is a vision of service to our people in the form of a cultural learning place that is founded in Biblical admonitions to remember God's blessings and "how we got over" during times of peril, lest we forget this history and lose our way. To paraphrase a verse from Proverbs 29:18, where there is no vision or knowledge of one's past, the people perish. Also, "diligently keep yourself, lest you forget the things your eyes have seen, and lest they depart from your heart all the days of your life. And teach them to your children and your grandchildren" (Deuteronomy 4:9).

In accepting the baton to lead the National Center through its formative years, I realize that I am standing on the shoulders of others, poised confidently to make my own contributions to preserve the legacy and place the National Center's activities on a firm foundation for the children yet unborn. I recall the writings of Ida B. Wells, who dedicated her autobiography, *Crusade for Justice,* to the young people that she felt had so little of their race history recorded (Wells 4). She felt this same imperative because there was such a lack of authentic race history of Reconstruction time written by the Negro him- or herself. As a result of her writings, we have a record of early lynchings and human injustices of this period to share with future generations. Similarly, the National Center seeks to fulfill the hopes of its early teachers and students who planned the movement for social change. They attended mass civil rights meetings, marched and boycotted the buses for equality, and left a rich legacy of contributions to civil rights. In the words of Dr. J. Garrick Hardy, Professor Emeritus of Sociology at ASU, in 1979:

I hope when history is recorded the world will know what part Alabama State played in the great Movement. Alabama State was the place where most of the planning sessions were held by Dr. Martin Luther King, Jr. I picked up people in the morning and evening as did most of the teachers and staff here at Alabama State. It caused us some problems but we continued to work diligently. (Interview with G. Garrick Hardy 7.)

To fulfill the dream of Dr. Hardy, ASU's contributions to the struggle will be recorded and celebrated in the National Center's mission.

We owe a great debt to our own historically black colleges and universities that provided a workplace for teachers like Dr. Hardy, who toiled selflessly to transmit and hold on to our culture. My own passion for my work at ASU is in keeping with feelings within me that these institutions are precious. For this reason, I feel an inherent obligation to make a difference within these walls. There is a rich culture at HBCUs and a genuine warmth in spite of the challenges that these institutions often face. In my own life, I understand that "to whom much is given, much is required" (Luke 12:48). As a graduate of a historically black university, I feel a real desire to give back to these schools and colleges that have been keepers of the record for so long. This desire to serve compels me to cherish the time that I have spent educating the "children coming on," as described by Dr. E. D. Nixon, father of the Montgomery bus boycott and contributor to our Center's archives. Teaching our children to understand their history goes beyond the normal assigned work responsibilities. These are the generations of children who know very little about our history, who often have low self-esteem, wandering in the wilderness of life, not knowing their own rich heritage and the possibility of a bright future. It is a special calling to which I have responded. Much is given, and much is, in turn, received for my own enrichment.

"Yet who knows whether you have come to the kingdom for such a time as this?" (Esther 4:14).

As children, it was expected of us, the offspring of black educators, to seek higher education and become leaders of our race as envisioned by W. E. B. Du Bois in his philosophy of the "talented tenth" (Simmons and Hutchinson 243). All of my grandmother's children during the early years of the twentieth century were products of historically black colleges and universities. They had been encouraged at a young age to become teachers, a profession that was highly regarded within the black community for the role educators played in uplifting their race after slavery. In the wise words of my grandmother, a second-generation teacher born in the late 1800s, "if you find anything better than working in the field of education, then go to it." In my own life, I could not "forfeit nature's claim," knowing full well that the path had already been laid for me to carry the torch as a fourth-generation member of the teaching profession. From these early influences, I have learned to appreciate the mission of HBCUs in transmitting the cultural heritage and preserving our glorious past as African Americans.

An inner drive for intellectual discovery was also fueled by my mother's influence as a school librarian; she understood and instilled in me the importance of keeping the historical record of our people—a people who had not valued or been taught to cherish their past. Having followed in her footsteps as not only a teacher but a second-generation librarian, I am continually inspired by the words of our elders, who remind us of the importance of keeping the record, of setting forth "truth" for truth's sake. Perhaps it is the knowledge of what we have lost in our past that challenges us to salvage what remains of our cultural heritage for our children.

As librarians at historically black schools and colleges, we understand the urgency to hold fast to our treasures, our records of black achievement. It has been the work of skilled librarians to preserve the stories of our victory "up from slavery," exemplified in the life of the great educator himself, Booker T. Washington, who documented his trials and hard-fought victories. Succeeding in spite of the odds against them, our early leaders, like Washington, built schools to educate the masses, lifting the veil of ignorance forced upon them during slavery. The stories must be preserved and retold to future generations. If we forget our history, we may be doomed to repeat the trials of our past or lose hope when we do not learn from the wisdom of our ancestors.

"And the Lord answered me, and said, write the vision, and make it plain upon tables, that he may run that readeth it" (Habakkuk 2:2).

What a glorious mission for our Center and for my work as a librarian and project director for this endeavor. Documenting these stories has revealed new truths applicable to my own life that sustain me during times requiring self-discipline, strength, love, and patience with my fellow man. It is my firm belief that throughout history, God has intervened to correct wrongs, to set a new course, and to create a new sense of balance and fair play. In this case, by giving to us the mission of a national research center at Alabama State University in Montgomery, the birthplace of the Confederacy and the modern civil rights movement, God has revealed himself yet again as the force that controls our past and our future for a better world. People around the world will be the beneficiary of this great history that we will preserve in our Center, thereby learning new lessons for new occasions to ensure freedom for all. Our Center for research will be realized as not just a museum or only a place to tour, but as a place to teach morals, lessons, and truth. It became my own resolve as I read again the words of Dr. King to ensure that the history books written in the future tell the whole story and inject new meaning into the veins of history and civilization, as envisioned by Dr. King.

Montgomery's people, with "fleecy locks and black complexion," stood together, united in their purpose, regardless of their station, to oppose oppression. They nonviolently brought about social change by this unity, and according to God's plan, their success did not hinge on any one person but was remembered as a people's movement orchestrated by God for his own glory. Looking back over the events of Montgomery, one can sense the majesty and mystery of it all. Here a people stood firm in their sacrifice for freedom, igniting a flame that has burned around the world for civil and human rights.

Establishing a research clearinghouse at ASU is most appropriate for teaching the values of a people who have survived against immeasurable odds. We work relentlessly in our Center, primarily as volunteers, committed to offering programs, seminars, outreach services, and scholarly publications that document, protect, and disseminate this valuable information. We sing the praises of the "unsung heroes" of the movement who have not sought or received credit for their enormous contributions.

The inception of the National Center is a watershed event in the history of Alabama State University. It will thrive because its mission preserves a vital part of American history as forecast by the National Endowment for the Humanities. With this intent by those of us who treasure the National Center's existence, it may one day become an International Center for the Study of Civil Rights and African-American Culture. In so doing, I, too, will realize my own personal quest to carry the torch for the preservation of truth and knowledge, not only for the uplift of black people, but for all mankind to learn the wisdom of freedom and justice for all. As Cowper wrote:

> Skins may differ, but affection
> Dwells in black and white the same.

PART TWO

Region-Wide
Seamless Fit

4 / I Go to College

Frank E. Moorer

I finished R. B. Hudson High School May 24, 1957, in Selma, Alabama. There were a hundred and thirty of us in the class of 1957. The occasion was on Friday night at seven in the school auditorium. It was a time of great anticipation for all of us. I had waited a long time for this moment, for I would be the first one of my siblings to graduate from high school. Only two members of my immediate family were there, my mother and a first cousin. Many close friends came, however. I had an older brother who would have graduated from Snow Hill Normal and Industrial Institute, but he had been drafted into the army during World War II, and when he returned, he was not well. In fact, he died on October 11, 1947. Thus, on one level, I would be graduating for both of us.

I had no idea about what I was going to do with my life after high school. In high school, I took the college prep course, but I did not have any money with which to attend college. One of my high school teachers—Mr. Harrison—made an effort to get me and some other young men into Knoxville College in Tennessee. In fact, he took us to visit the college one weekend, and he also made an effort to help us find work during the summer so that we would be able to attend college in the fall. He did not have to do this; he did it on his own, simply because he wanted to help some young black men get a college education.

As I look back from the vantage point of forty-four years, the trip was a memorable one because it was only my third time outside of Alabama. We took the trip to Knoxville during the spring vacation of 1957. Mr. Harrison took the time for us to stop in Chattanooga, Tennessee, where we visited Lookout Mountain. There were three other young men on the trip: Josephus Wesly, Robert Lilly, and, I believe, Smiley. (I do not recall his first name.)

I returned from Knoxville with college on my mind. As seniors, recruiters from many of the historically black colleges had visited our school and talked to us about attending their respective colleges. So, I had an idea of what was involved in going to college. I applied to three colleges: Knoxville, Morehouse, and Oakwood, and I was accepted by all three.

Oakwood was the only Alabama school that I applied to. I had known about this small Seventh-day Adventist College in Huntsville all my life. Because my aunt, Lula V. Moorer, sent the college a twenty-five dollar donation, the college sent her a yearbook, which she highly prized. The pictures of the students in the yearbook impressed me, too.

In the meantime, school was out, and I went from the tiny hamlet, Pink's Bottom, where we lived, to Birmingham, looking for a job. I went to live with my sister Lillie Pearl and her husband—without alerting them to the fact that I was coming. They were living in Washington Park near our cousins, Gertrude (Henderson) and Frank Robinson. I did not find a job that summer, but I did grow up some. For example, I tried to drive my brother-in-law's 1951 Chevrolet, and I was doing pretty well until I tried to turn a corner. As I was turning the corner, I ran up on the sidewalk and hit a new, parked Buick. My brother-in-law, Jesse Moultrie, paid for the damages.

I did look for a job, but I could not find one. I am sure I was looking in the wrong places. And too, I had no concept of what would be involved in working at a full-time job. I had had one job while in high school, washing dishes and cleaning up the kitchen at the Officers Club on Craig Air Force Base in Selma. Thus in the summer of 1957, I was incredibly naive about the larger society in general and work in particular. Yet I was no stranger to work, for I had grown up in rural Dallas County, working on farms, chopping and picking cotton, and doing many other tasks. I just did not know how to go about finding a job in what for me was a large city.

Birmingham was also a segregated city. I did not think about the segregation too much because I simply wanted a job that would pay enough to allow me to attend college that fall; that did not happen. I returned to Selma. Later, in the summer, I wrote Oakwood College about working during the summer. The college gave me a job. I borrowed five dollars from Mama

Cindy, a family member, and with much trepidation, I took a Trailways bus to Huntsville, Alabama. Because I had no money and very few clothes, I was in no hurry for the bus to arrive in Huntsville. When I arrived there in the summer of 1957, it was a small southern town. Huntsville would begin its phenomenal growth during the two plus years that I spent at Oakwood College. So I went to college without any resources; I worked that summer and the first semester in the Oakwood College Laundry and Dry Cleaning in order to take my first college classes in the spring of 1958.

As noted above, Oakwood is a Seventh-day Adventist College; it was founded in 1896 to educate black members of the church who wanted an education in a Christian environment. When I arrived, it had been a senior college for about seventeen years. I must say that to my eighteen-year-old eyes, the college campus was beautiful. It was, to be sure, what I needed at the time. Coming from a small rural community in Dallas County, Alabama, I had no conception of what a college was like, for my high school teachers had not fully prepared me for college. I had done very little writing in high school, so I knew nothing about writing essays. I also had no concept of sentence structure and paragraph development. In a word, I was lost. Because the college was small, I got some of the attention that I needed. Therefore, in going to college, I had taken my first steps toward becoming an educated man.

The late 1950s were a time of change in the African American community and the larger society. The Montgomery bus boycott of 1955–1956 ushered in the direct-action nonviolent phase of the modern civil rights movement. The boycott showed what a united black community could do to change the dynamics of race—even in the South, for, apart from the victory of integrated buses in Montgomery, the Montgomery boycott changed the black community's sense of itself and its power. In the process of struggling to integrate buses, black people realized that by pooling their courage, they could overcome their fear of the white power structure and improve their lives in the process. While we were aware, as Oakwood College students, of what was going in the larger society, we were by and large insulated from the struggles of the larger society.

Even though we were not directly engaged in the civil rights struggle, the college did open another world for me. I was, for the first time, introduced to blacks from Africa as well as from the diaspora—from West and southern Africa and from the many islands in the West Indies and from South and

Central America. In this instance, the college extended my small, rural, Alabama world to a global one. I became interested in Africa—especially the Gold Coast whose name was changed to Ghana in 1957, at the time of its independence. I also met two young black men, David and William Robinson, who had lived in Uganda. They made Africa a real presence for me.

The college also brought structure to my life and the lives of others. Life at Oakwood was highly regimented. We had morning and evening worship services five days a week. Morning worship was brief; it started at 6:45 and ended ten minutes later. Evening worship services were more extensive, lasting from 6:30 to 7:15 p.m., Sunday through Thursday. In addition to the worship services in the dorms and the chapel services, we had to attend vespers service every Friday evening. I especially enjoyed the vesper services because we learned a lot of new hymns, and the singing during vespers service was wonderful. Finally, on Saturday, the Sabbath, every student was required to attend church services, and attend we did. Because the eleven o'clock services were well planned, I enjoyed most of them. Happily, since the college administrators knew what students were like, the eleven o'clock worship services seldom went beyond 12:30.

Like most private black colleges at the time, Oakwood had compulsory chapel three times per week. I am sure at the time I somewhat resented chapel, yet I learned much about the outside world during those hours, for the college made a serious effort to introduce us to a wide spectrum of ideas. The term "compulsory" was backed up by a fine: if a student had more than three unexcused chapel absences during a semester, he/she had to pay a dollar for each absence beyond those three—and in 1958 a dollar was a lot of money, so most of us attended each chapel session.

Oakwood also required all students to attend its lyceum series. For me, the lyceum programs were an education in themselves. The school brought in outstanding talent—singers, concert pianists, and lecturers. During my two plus years at the college, I heard Phillipa Schuyler in a piano concert, Neal Douglas lecturing on Russia, and a black man (whose name I cannot recall at the moment) on African culture. I also heard for the first time the Christmas sections of Handel's *Messiah*. The Oakwood College Choir, along with members of the larger community, presented the program each year. Something in the tenor aria "Comfort Ye, Comfort Ye My People" resonated with me, and even now the aria is still one of my favorites. All of this was extending my small world. I was learning in and out of the classroom.

I also made good friends at Oakwood College. I recall Tommy Bedgood from the Mississippi Delta. We shared an interest in black history in general and the history of black colleges in particular. We called each other Jackson after the president of the National Baptist Convention, the Reverend Joseph Jackson. Bedgood was majoring in religion. I believe he saw me as a kindred spirit. I also met one of my closest friends, Charles McCellan from Chicago, a very smart and kind young man. Charles, I believe, was also a kindred spirit. We took long walks; the college was blessed with a more than a thousand acres of land. Sometimes, we had a small picnic in the woods. We talked about the school and the larger world. There were also other friends, male and female, that made my experience at Oakwood very rewarding.

I left Oakwood in the fall of 1960 because I did not have money to pay my fees. I never returned as a student, but I returned for visits from time to time. The last time I saw my friend Charles McCellan was during one of those visits back to Oakwood, in 1961. We took our usual walk, and we also had a picnic. We enjoyed each other's company. After I left the college, I wrote Charles a few times, and I am sure he responded, but somehow, we lost touch with each other.

The next time that I had news of Charles, I was living in Atlanta, Georgia, attending Atlanta University in 1963–64. I was told one Sabbath, at the Seventh-day Adventist Church, by a young lady from Chicago who knew Charles very well—I knew her, too, from my Oakwood days—that Charles had returned to Chicago and later committed suicide. I was deeply hurt. On one occasion, Charles had asked to go home with me. I do not recall how I responded. I knew Charles had a brother, but I never got in touch with him after Charles's death. I am still at a loss because I do not know what drove Charles to take his life. He was a loving person. And yet, I did not really know what he wanted in life. We never talked about our fears and hopes. We never discussed girls. In fact, we did not talk about sex at all. After these many years, I can still see Charles's smile.

I also had some very fine teachers at Oakwood College. My history teacher Mr. Murray Harvey Sr. made history real to me and to the other freshmen who took his European Civilization class. As I now look back, I realize that we were not taught anything about the history of black people in this country. We were taught about dead Europeans and Americans who really had no bearing on our daily lives. I came to college with a deep interest in what in 1957 was called Negro history that had been nurtured by my high school American history teacher, Mr. Votie M. Anderson. Even though he did not talk about Negro and African history at Oakwood, I found in Mr. Harvey an inspiring teacher. Mr. Harvey made me believe that I could aspire to become a college teacher. He shattered the image of the African American inscribed in the culture as an absence, someone who had no control of his/her life; instead, he (re)inscribed an image of the African American self as professional, an image that I sorely needed in 1958. He, along with other teachers at Oakwood, invited students to their homes, thereby making us feel that we were truly a part of the college.

When I arrived at Oakwood in the fall of 1957, I had no real grasp of the English language. Thus, I was not equipped for my first year of college English. I was very fortunate to have a good English teacher, Ms. L. Henrietta Emanuel, who was a gruff but kind woman. She was well grounded in her field, and she knew how to impart knowledge to her students—even to me, despite my lack of preparation. I was always terrified that I would be called on in class and would not know the answer. I did not know how to begin writing an essay because we wrote no essays in high school. And yet, I cannot use that as an excuse. I needed to study, and I also needed a lot of hands-on teaching.

I had two other inspiring teachers during my Oakwood years. Ms. Natelkka Burrell taught me educational psychology, and it was she who made it possible for me to attend a National Education Association conference at the University of Kansas during the summer of 1959. This was the first time I left the South. I did enjoy my visit to Lawrence, Kansas. It was also my first time in an integrated situation. The final Oakwood teacher who made an impact on me was Elder Giddings, who had served as a missionary for the Seventh-day Aventist Church in Liberia, West Africa, for ten years. He taught me geography and the history of American education. It was the geography class that expanded my horizons. He made us aware of the profound racial problems in South Africa, and he taught us about other parts of Africa as well. In his teaching, he constantly encouraged us to learn other languages (he spoke French and Spanish) and to travel as well. Elder Giddings also enhanced my knowledge of West Africa, the West Indies, and South America.

I left Oakwood College after two plus years. I believe I was a bit wiser, but I was far from being a well-educated young man. Oakwood College opened up a larger world for me, and the religious life of the college made a profound impression on me; we were taught that the intellectual and religious life should complement each other, and that religion should be an integral part of the Christian's everyday existence. The lyceum programs were also mind expanding. I had left Pink's Bottom and Selma a very rural young man; Oakwood College made me aware of how much I did not know and of the need to read and educate myself. I returned to Selma to live, where I remained for a year reading and working as a substitute teacher in Dallas County. I also did a brief stint as a construction worker.

During the spring semester of 1961, I attended Selma University, another black college, this one founded in 1878 by black Baptists. At the time, Selma University was little more than a junior college. And yet, the semester that I spent there was not wasted. I entered into the life of this small school with vigor. I made some very good friends. Frank Smith from Lower Peach Tree, Alabama, became my closest friend. He later graduated from Morehouse College and Morehouse School of Religion. We remained friends until his death in an automobile accident some years later. While still a student at Selma University, I wrote the admissions office at Rust College in Holly Springs, Mississippi, for an application and a catalog. I soon received both. After studying the catalog and noting that the school was not very expensive, I applied for admission. I knew little about Rust College; in fact, I first heard about Rust College from Solomon Outlaw, a fellow student from Mississippi, while I was still at Oakwood. Since I did not have any prospects of getting a good job during the summer of 1961, I requested employment at Rust. Once I was accepted, I was offered a job for the summer, which I accepted.

My main problem was how to get there. I did not have any money at the time. I could not expect any help from my father because he was not interested in my getting a college education. Of his nine children, none of us had finished college. I did have about thirty dollars due me from the construction job, which I used to buy a footlocker and a few clothes. A friend, Edward O. Jones, was going to Jackson, Tennessee, that summer to help the Seventh-day Adventists with a tent effort (revival). En route to Jackson, he stopped at Oakwood for the Seventh-day Adventist South Central Conference's camp meeting. As I reflect on the experience, I believe Edward said that I could ride with him to Jackson. He also noted that Holly Springs, Mississippi, was not too far from Jackson.

I did ride up to Oakwood with Edward that weekend, and I was able to visit some old friends at the college. We talked about my new college. While

I definitely enjoyed my visit, I also had feelings of anxiety about going to Mississippi, an unknown quantity for me. Even though I had spent all of my life in Alabama, which was teeming with racism, we still viewed Mississippi as the very bottom of the heap for our people. My Aunt Estelle Moorer Sewell, my father's sister, said, "I heard that in some places in Mississippi, Negroes have to put their heads in a barrel to laugh because white folks don't allow them to laugh in public." She made the statement with a great deal of concern in her voice. And she further asked: "Frank Edward, you ain't going to that part of Mississippi, is you, boy?" I did not know what to say, yet here I was on my way to Rust College in northern Mississippi. If I had not gone to Mississippi, I did not, at that time, have anywhere else to go. I was not sure that I was making the right decision. Certainly, I did not have the money to return to Oakwood. I did not even have the money to pay my way to Rust, let alone have bus fare back home in the event I did not like the school. So I just went, hoping everything would fall in place. It did.

We left Oakwood on a late Sunday afternoon in June 1961, heading for Jackson. The trip was new because I had not been to the northwest section of Alabama or to western Tennessee. As we drew closer to Jackson, I became increasingly uneasy because I did not have any money on me at all. I would, however, need bus fare from Jackson, Tennessee, to Holly Springs, Mississippi. Once in Jackson, I simply said, "Edward, I don't have any money for bus fare from here to Holly Springs. Will you please lend me five dollars?" "Yes," he said, and I thank him to this day. Someone took me down to the Greyhound bus station, where I purchased a ticket for Holly Springs. After the purchase, I believe I had a dollar and a half left. It was well past midnight when the bus arrived in Memphis. At the bus station, I spent fifty cents for food, which left me one dollar, and changed buses. Early Monday morning, I was on the last leg of my journey to Rust College. The bus soon left Tennessee, and I was in Mississippi—the state where, according to the late Reverend Harry Richardson, the devil lived. The bus stopped in a number of small towns before arriving in Holly Springs. As the bus entered Holly Springs, I could see the imposing administration building on the Rust College campus, which looked very much like Independence Hall in Philadelphia. The Greyhound bus soon stopped at a store serving as a bus station. Since it was early in the morning, the town was still asleep. I felt ill at ease because I was in a new place. What would the college be like? How would I fit in?

A lone taxicab waited at the bus station. "How much will it cost to take me to Rust College?" I asked. "One dollar," the cab driver replied. That one dollar was all the money I had in the world. I was more than three hundred miles from Selma. What was even more disconcerting, I did not know anyone in Holly Springs. I was indeed a stranger in a very strange place. I knew I had to do well at this new college to earn my keep.

The campus was small and beautiful. The imposing administration building was in the center of the campus. The other buildings were shabby compared to it. The campus, however, was clean. Since it was still too early for the office to be open, I walked around the campus. My walk was very short. I returned to the side of the administration building near McDonald Hall to wait until the Office of Student Affairs opened. As I stood waiting, nearly every student who passed spoke. Some even introduced themselves. They wanted to know where I was from, and they reminded me that I was too late for the first summer session. "I'm here to work this summer in order to attend school in the fall. I'm not here for summer school," I noted.

At eight o'clock, I went up to the office of Mr. E. T. Battle, the director of student affairs. His secretary, Ms. Rubye Collins, was very friendly, and her warm attitude made me feel at ease. I was soon ushered into Mr. Battle's office. He was also kind and helpful. "Yes," he noted, "we had expected you to be here at the beginning of the month. You will work with Mr. Griffin, the superintendent of buildings and grounds, this summer. You will stay in McDonald Hall, and you will take your meals in the cafeteria. All the money that you make this summer will go towards your tuition for the fall," he said. I thanked Mr. Battle, left his office, and went to find my room in McDonald Hall.

My room on the second floor was bare and scruffy with dirty, off-white walls. There were two iron bunk beds, a chair, a large desk, and a closet. The room had two large windows and a single light bulb that gave off a somewhat weak yellow light. While the accommodations were not as nice as the ones at Oakwood College, I was glad to have a job, a roof over my head, three meals a day, and the prospect of completing my education. I also fell in love with this rather small and struggling college.

From the middle of June to the end of August 1961, I worked full time on the campus doing a variety of jobs. My first job was walking across the campus with a sack and pick, picking up trash. I did this for about a week. My next job was picking up garbage from the faculty homes. Frederick

Brown helped me collect garbage; he later became a minister in the United Methodist Church. The final summer jobs were painting E. L. Rust Hall and cleaning dorm rooms for the fall. At the end of each week, we were given four dollars for spending money. I saved most of mine. I met some good people that summer. Johnny Anthony, who remained a friend for many years, was one such person, majoring in music. Williefene Sykes, a young woman majoring in English education, and I discussed Sidney Lanier's "Marshes of Glynn." She went on to teach English in the Arkansas public schools.

During the two years I spent at Rust College, I worked in the library to pay my tuition and other fees. I was paid the princely sum of eight hundred dollars per semester, which covered all of my school fees, and I had a little money left over. Working in the library expanded my education. I worked in every part of our small library, and I especially enjoyed working in the reference area. In order to help the students and faculty, I had to know the collection. Therefore, during my spare time, I read the shelves in the main reading room. I also dipped into the many reference sources, learning how to use them. I started reading the *New York Times* in 1961, especially the Sunday edition and the book review section. In addition to reading the *Times,* I began to read the *New Yorker,* and one of the essays that I read in the magazine was James Baldwin's "Letter from a Region in My Mind." Needless to say, I was deeply impressed with Baldwin as a prose writer. I also read other black writers while working in the library—Richard Wright, Langston Hughes, and Zora Neale Hurston.

Working in the library forced me to be an adult, which I was in terms of age, but I was given added responsibility: I had to open and close the library. It was during this time that I decided to study for a graduate degree in library service. Thus, in my senior year, I applied to the Atlanta University School of Library Service. I was accepted and given a full tuition scholarship.

Unlike Oakwood, Rust College was not accredited, but there were some very fine teachers at the college. Mr. E. T. Battle, who was in drama, did not allow the lack of an auditorium to keep him from presenting excellent plays. I still remember his productions of Lorraine Hansberry's *A Raisin in the Sun* and Langston Hughes's *Simply Heavenly,* outdoors behind the administration building. Mrs. Frances N. Eaton, probably the most outstanding teacher at Rust, taught economics. She was a native Mississippian who had graduated from Rust College in 1915. After graduation, she went to Northwestern University to study for a degree in music. She taught music and directed the Rust College Choir for many years. She was a proud, light-brown-skinned woman of average height and build, who always dressed well. She did not accept Mississippi's racial mores, however. In fact, she resisted any form of racial proscription. Because she refused to smile for the whites when the choir sang for them, Dr. McCoy, the president of Rust College at the time, encouraged her to leave music. I am glad she did. She returned to Northwestern and studied economics. She earned a master's in the field in the 1940s and returned to Rust where she remained until her death in 1967.

Mrs. Eaton was an excellent teacher by any standard. She loved imparting knowledge to young black men and women. She lectured on the American economy in particular and the plight of black people in general. She also taught American economic history and international relations. She knew her subjects well. Because she was so well grounded in her field, she insisted that we had the capacity to be outstanding students, too. She not only taught economics, but she also taught us how to survive in Mississippi with a modicum of dignity. I can still see her now, after forty years, standing before her class lecturing on the American economy as a mixed capitalist one, and suddenly stopping to say, "Do not smile at any white person in uptown Holly Springs. Do not show them your teeth. I refuse to give them my complete name. I simply sign myself as F. N. Eaton," and she would add, "Only my friends call me Frances." She made it clear that even in 1960s Mississippi, we had to let those in power know that we did not like the system under which we lived.

Mrs. Eaton also encouraged her students to do graduate work at northern universities. She taught me to love my subject and my love for teaching; because she was such a bright light in dark Mississippi, I will always cherish her memory. Her example more than any other teacher, with the possible exception of my high school history teacher, Mr. Votie M. Anderson, had a profound influence on my career choice to become a college teacher. She encouraged us to believe in ourselves, and she insisted that we must not be satisfied with a degree from Rust. Rather, we should study for a doctoral degree in our respective fields. I well remember that she encouraged me and Leslie B. McLemore, who currently teaches political science at Jackson State University in Mississippi and who received his PhD in political science from the University of Massachusetts, to go to Atlanta University for our master's degrees or for a year of graduate study before we applied to a northern university for further study. She felt that this black graduate school would get us ready for the demanding task of PhD study, and on that point she was correct. I am sure if Mrs. F. N. Eaton had not been such a fine teacher who believed in our potential, I would not have gone to graduate school. She shattered the dominant image of African Americans inscribed in the larger society as "shiftless head-scratching darkies"; instead, she reinscribed the image of black men and women as proud human beings and professionals.

The college president, Dr. E. A. Smith, a native of Birmingham, Alabama, was also an outstanding individual and a great speaker. He graduated from Rust College in 1937. After graduation, he studied theology at Oberlin College and the Hartford Seminary foundation. Before returning to Rust, he had taught school and pastored a number of United Methodist churches. He gave us the benefit of his vast experiences in his chapel addresses. He introduced us to Søren Kierkegaard and to existentialism and opened our minds to possibilities beyond Mississippi. He also encouraged students to participate in the civil rights struggle. In fact, during my senior year, he led a civil rights march in uptown Holly Springs. There were also many other fine people at the college who made Rust such a nurturing landscape.

One of the other good things about my experience at Rust College was the civil rights movement. The echoes of the struggle were everywhere in Mississippi. Students at the college had boycotted the local movie house. I met Frank Smith, a SNCC field secretary, in Mississippi in 1962, and Robert Moses, who was also working with SNCC in Mississippi. In fact Frank, who became my roommate, introduced me to SNCC, and I attended my first conference in Nashville at Fisk University in the fall of 1962. It was in Nashville that I met Bernice Johnson who later married Cordell Reagan. She was the first person I ever saw with an "Afro." She later organized Sweet Honey in the Rock, a female vocal group. We also had an NAACP chapter on campus organized by Medgar Evers. The college made it clear to each of us that we had the power to help change the society, that is, if we believed in ourselves.

At Rust College, I was even more involved in student activities than I had been at Oakwood. I was active in the student government and the campus Sunday school. During my senior year, I became superintendent of the Sunday school. Along with other students, I encouraged black people to register to vote. I even ran for student government president for the term 1962–63.

I lost that election, but I did become the president of the senior class. I graduated from Rust College on May 28, 1963, with a major in secondary education. Two years prior, I had arrived at Rust with nothing but a foot-locker and a few clothes. Now I was leaving with my BS degree and with a number of good friends.

The only member of my family who came to the ceremony was my dear mother, Mrs. Leanna Andrews Moorer. She and a cousin were the only ones who had attended my high school graduation. Looking back on the experience, for some unknown reason, I was ashamed of my dear and wonderful mother. She did not have to come, but she did. Yet here I was, a half-educated young fool ashamed of this loving woman who was glad that I had finished college—something that she had not been able to do, given the times in which she lived, and she rejoiced that one of her children had finished high school and college. I have thought about this for years, and I cannot come up with a satisfactory answer—or I simply do not want to admit that I was a shallow young man.

There were also fine people in the community that made my stay at Rust College a rewarding one. Mr. O. C. and Mrs. Velma Peagus were my ideal of what a married couple should be. They were hardworking and God-fearing people, members of the Calvin Chapel United Methodist Church. They had nine well-disciplined children. All of the children finished high school, and most of them attended college. This couple did not allow Mississippi to kill their spirit. I enjoyed many fine meals at their home. They were also at my graduation.

I am glad I went to Rust College in the summer of 1961, for it proved to be an excellent place for growing. Since I was a long way from Selma, Alabama, I had to make friends in order to survive. The very journey put me on the road to taking charge of my own life. I made a number of good friends, and I did survive. I realized that to accomplish something I had to begin and work until it was completed. In the process of completing my undergraduate education, I made Rust College and Mississippi an integral part of my intellectual and personal world/landscape. For Rust College started me on the road to becoming a college professor, and it also helped me and others to shatter the negative image of black people that was held in the larger society. The college taught me and others that we could project our own image onto history. In fact, I came to love Mississippi.

While Rust College did not have all the facilities and equipment that made a good college, the spirit of the school and the faculty made up for the lack of the resources. I mentioned earlier that the college was not accredited by the Southern Association of Colleges and Schools. It was, however, approved by the Mississippi Department of Education for training teachers. Because Rust College saw itself as a part of the struggle for racial equality, students were encouraged to participate in voter registration, in the NAACP, in SNCC, and in other organizations. The college also had a very fine a cappella choir.

I entered Atlanta University in the fall of 1963 to study for the MS in Library Service. Atlanta University was the graduate school in the Atlanta University Center. The teachers in the School of Library Service were excellent. The Trevor Arnett Library had an excellent collection on black history and culture. I was able to read widely in African American history and literature. One of my teachers in the library school, Mrs. Josephine Thompson, had been a student of W. E. B. Du Bois, and she often talked about him.

To a young black man from small-town Mississippi and rural Alabama, the Atlanta University Center offered wonderful opportunities for growth. For instance, there was a year-long lecture series on Africa. In addition to the series on Africa, Atlanta University sponsored a Town Hall Forum. One of the speakers for the Forum was Louis Lomax, an outstanding African American journalist. Dr. Martin Luther King Jr. spoke at Morehouse; I refused to go hear him because I did not believe in hero worship. If I had known at the time that I would later work at the M. L. King Center for Nonviolent Social Change, I would have gone. I also attended my first Shakespeare production, *Hamlet,* at Clark College that year.

I was able to continue my interest and connection with SNCC. The home office was located at 6½ Raymond Street, a mere two blocks from my dormitory. Of course, I was a frequent visitor at the office. I already knew Ruby Doris Smith, the office manager. She would later become the executive secretary of SNCC. I even took part in a protest at the First Baptist Church. Nearly every Sunday for almost an academic term, we marched with our signs in front of the church, reminding the congregation that it was not being Christian by keeping blacks out. Our main goal at the time, however, was to reduce the bond of the Reverend Ashton Jones, who had taken some black people with him to the church. The whole group was arrested and put in jail. Their bail was, I believe, set at twenty thousand dollars. Reverend Jones refused to pay it; thus, he was in jail. We felt the bond was much too high. As a result of our protest, Reverend Jones was released from jail and the church opened its doors to black people.

Atlanta University also had in place programs in reading and English to help those of us who needed them. I needed both. Mrs. Lucy Clemmons Grisby was the teacher for English Composition; she was not only an excellent teacher, but also a first-rate human being. I remained in touch with her until her death in 1999. By the time I left Atlanta University, I knew I would get a PhD. The university gave me the opportunity to take control of my own education and to receive a fine education in library service. In sum, the excellent special collection on black American history and culture, the fine lecture series on Africa, the Town Hall Forum, and the support services expanded my knowledge and gave me the confidence that I needed to be a professional librarian and to continue my education at a northern university.

Without historically black colleges, then, I would not have been able to attend college at all. In the first place, I did not have the financial resources, and, in terms of academics, I was not adequately prepared for such an adventure. These colleges, however, took me where I was and pushed me into becoming a better student, making it possible for me to become a professional librarian and, finally, a college professor—at another historically black institution, Alabama State University.

5 / Living a Womanist Legacy

Elaine M. Smith

"When Martin Luther King started the Montgomery Bus Boycott—"
"What?" I interrupted, as if to stop a crime. "King didn't *start* the boy-cott," I explained. "The Women's Political Council did!" The student in my Alabama State University World History class nodded acquiescence as he went on to laud King's leadership in the 1955–56 boycott.

This seemingly insignificant exchange reminded me of comments made about seventy-five years ago by legendary educator-activist Mary McLeod Bethune. "The work of men is heralded and adorned, while that of women is given last place or entirely overlooked," she observed. Nonetheless, Bethune encouraged women onward: "We must go to the front and take our rightful place; fight our battles and claim our victories" (Smith 149).

Much has changed in the status of African American women since both Bethune's day and the Montgomery bus boycott. A few years ago U.S. Sena-tor Carol Mosely Braun, an Illinois Democrat, symbolized the heights now accessible to black women. Condoleezza Rice, the Secretary of State under President George W. Bush, and Oprah Winfrey, corporate institution and talk-show diva, do the same today.

While such advances are encouraging, the truth in an old adage should be acknowledged: "The more things change, the more they remain the same." African American women suffer still from discrimination stemming primarily from a duality of sources—gender and race. A useful term sub-suming both is *womanism,* as opposed to the more singularly focused "feminism." Womanism carries the idea of black women grappling with both female and race problems and their derivatives, while not automatically castigating black men. Certainly in Alabama, women must traverse a great distance to gain equality. Among all the states, it has the highest percentage of women who have not completed high school; the highest wage differential between men and women; and the lowest percentage of women in a state legislature. Additionally, its Congressional delegation is devoid of women.

Routinely, I witness women's less-than-equal status in voluntary associations, particularly the black church. In 2001, for example, when St. John's Working Club celebrated "A Century of Service," marking its first hundred years as an auxiliary in St. John's (the most prominent African Methodist Episcopal [AME] Church in Montgomery), local civil rights legend, well-known ASU professor-emeritus, and club president Thelma Glass presented to the church a plaque with the name of every woman in the club during its hundred-year history. She did so "as an inspiration and motivation [to others] to do God's work" ("Special Presentations"). The cooperative and gracious pastor accepted the plaque—and promptly consigned it to a basement room rarely visited. I have not seen it since and hardly anybody else has either. The point is that although black women contribute mightily to community institutions, their efforts are often forgotten, ignored, or devalued. It is frequently true in narratives of male-female institutions. For example, the official historical sketch of St. John's Church at one hundred thirty years was essentially the parade of pastors, all male, who have occupied the pulpit. In this and other ways that usually cause scant reflection, black women endure gender bias.

Concurrently they confront race too, as my Montgomery experiences illustrate. Twenty-some years ago, my family lived in a middle-income, ninety-five percent white neighborhood. While we are still in the same house, the neighborhood is now ninety-five percent black. Emblematic of our original neighbors' attitude toward us was their children's refusal to play with our son. A more immediate illustration, however, involves my workplace, ASU, a historically black university originating during the Reconstruction Era. The local media and the corporate and governmental establishment, along with white Alabama, favor and grant disproportionate support to Auburn University-Montgomery, created in the 1960s under Governor George Wallace to duplicate ASU offerings and located on the other side of Montgomery. Seemingly, the powers that be continue to distrust the ability of African Americans to operate quality programs. Not all historically black colleges and universities exist in somewhat hostile cities, but then few other cities can claim historic civil rights symbolism on par with the Montgomery bus boycott and the Selma-to-Montgomery march.

While living with imposed race-gender biases, I have held membership in broad local and state organizations of varying race-gender configurations. One such organization is made up of black and white women, namely, the Montgomery Newcomers Club. Another type of organization is composed of black and white men and women, for I have served in the Montgomery County Historical Society, the Alabama Historical Association, and the Board of Directors for the Friends of the Alabama Archives. A third type consists essentially of black men and women, as do the St. John's AME Church and the Black Heritage Council, an advisory body of the Alabama Historical Commission.

Nevertheless, most of my time in voluntary associations is spent in womanist circles derived from an era when black women infrequently exercised creative leadership in other adult organizations. I appreciate the history behind them. They tie me to the woman on whom I have focused my professional research, Mary McLeod Bethune (1875–1955). Her greatest political underpinnings were womanist groups, including the National Association of Colored Women, founded in 1896, although she is more intimately identified with the organization she created in 1935, the National Council of Negro Women. I support especially needy voluntary associations that perpetuate a unique cultural heritage, because too often as blacks have desegregated historically white institutions, the institutions of their fathers and mothers have withered. In maintaining a cultural infrastructure, African Americans are positioned to invite others to integrate with them as they serve the community.

Although I am a member of a national sorority, my womanist organizational experience in Montgomery has been in club work—work that encompasses the so-called little things of life, easily forgotten, which nonetheless make for comfort and wholeness. I have enjoyed membership in Montgomery's Boylan-Haven Alumni, a loose network of about eight women who in high school attended the now-closed Methodist boarding school for girls in Jacksonville, Florida. It gathers irregularly today, but my three other womanist groups meet like clockwork: a church society, a civic club, and a federation embracing that club and other clubs. Civil rights luminary Coretta Scott King belonged to the latter two organizations when she lived in Montgomery while her husband pastored Dexter Avenue Baptist Church. These are community-focused organizations. Most womanist associations have been so, according to historian Gerda Lerner in her 1972 precedent-setting *Black Women in White America.* She observed, "If there is one theme that can emerge from the documentary record . . . it is the strength, racial pride and sense of community of black women" (xxv). In 1946, this strength, pride, and community spirit led Mary Fair Burks, an ASU English professor, to organize the Women's Political Council, which later, under ASU English professor Jo Ann Robinson, started the famed bus boycott. While the council no longer exists, other womanist networks in Alabama's capital city possess a storied past.

My three organizations lay claim to such a past. I believe that their stability is rooted in part in the longevity of the Montgomery black community, which extends back to the pre-Civil War era. Exercising a degree of group independence after the war, blacks established their own churches and other community concerns. The traditions of cooperation derived from this time prevailed until well into the civil rights period. Given the severely restricted sphere that racial segregation imposed upon people of color, it could not have been otherwise. That sphere was contracted in 1901, when white lawmakers in Alabama constitutionally disfranchised blacks. In that same year, just a few blocks from the Alabama capitol, the St. John's Working Club was established in its namesake church. Its distinctiveness centers in self-determination, for it has never been part of a denomination-wide organization; and in longevity, having existed for a century. Conversely, its activities and significance typify a multitude of small, unheralded—and sometimes invisible—church groups composed of women. The Working Club's name originated in a commitment to work for the church so that it could meet recurring financial obligations, including AME General Conference Claims. In August 1902, for example, the club donated $6.50 to the church's third-quarter income of $474.83. It persevered over eight decades in systematically contributing ever-increasing amounts until 1984, when the church, under Reverend Anderson Todd, effected a landmark financial reorganization based upon *individual* pledges. Freed from incessant fundraising, the club maintains a closely knit fellowship worthy of emulation,

characterized by members' concern for and loyalty to each other and virtually one hundred percent cooperation in every club endeavor. It affirms and
encourages members of the congregation, particularly in times of major
transitions including illnesses and deaths in the family. And it helps to perpetuate its beloved church as an institution through members' attending
most church functions, giving gifts to the church when asked and on its own
initiative, and in cultivating members' interest in the church through up-
dates on general church activities and services to members.

While the reach of the Working Club is limited to one congregation, my
civic unit, the Anna M. Duncan Club, impacts a wider field. Club organizer
Anna Duncan (1854–1903), an attractive Swayne School teacher, was "a
woman of rare ability and wonderful personality, loved and admired by all
who knew her" ("Origins"). In late September in 1897, at her home at 418
Montgomery Street, she began the organization, called during her life the
Twentieth Century Club, but later renamed to honor her. Its objectives
were to stimulate cultural programs, civic pride, and charity. Anna Duncan and other early members suffused these objectives with a passion to do
God's work, for they made little distinction between the secular and the
religious.

In virtually every meeting today the club song, whose author is no longer
known, sung to the tune of the "Battle Hymn of the Republic," reminds
members of the past. It speaks of typical necessities of Duncan sisters, including educating the race, earning a living, sponsoring positive outreach,
championing Biblical standards, and living zestfully. It refers to organizational mission, the unique position of African Americans as a challenged
minority, the historic, ascriptive limitations of their members relative to
other women, and the promise of transcendence. Consider these lyrics:

We are a band of women, from the ranks of life we come,
We are marching into battle though we've neither fife nor drum,
It shall ever be our motto, lifting others as we climb,
As we go marching on!

Our race must be enlightened, we must earn our daily bread,
We must give our time and talent and the hungry must be fed,
We must root out sin and sadness, planting good and joy instead,
As we go marching on!

All hail the Duncan women and may others join our band,
May the torch that we have lighted shine forever on our land,
Til the women of all races will be glad to take our hand,
As we go marching on!

Lifting others is our motto,
Lifting others is our motto,
Lifting others is our motto,
We're lifting as we climb.

Like scores of other local units in the country, the Anna M. Duncan Society was the early muscle for the National Association of Colored Women. Moreover, the club spearheaded the creation of the Alabama Association of Colored Women's Clubs here in Montgomery on December 29, 1899. Also, it has supplied the state organization with three presidents: Anna M. Duncan, 1899–1901; slave-born national education luminary Cornelia Bowen, 1905–1918; and Henrietta M. Gibbs, 1936–1943. Bowen, in particular, contributed to the signature achievement of the state organization: the opening in Mt. Meigs, Alabama, of a home for delinquent African American boys in 1908; and in 1919–20, a facility for girls on property adjacent to the boys' home. These two facilities have evolved into the Mt. Meigs Campus Complex of the Alabama Department of Youth Services, previously named the Alabama Industrial School. Travelers to Montgomery on Interstate 85 may glimpse this expansive property, purchased by clubwomen and given to the state, as they near the Montgomery city limits.

Forty years after the state association had begun, Montgomery women created a citywide network named the Montgomery City Federation of Colored Women's Clubs. Organized in the First Congregation Church, it unified twenty-five adult clubs and five youth clubs. It aspired to elevate the community in the areas of citizenship, family living, women and youth opportunities, and race relations. Today composed of eleven clubs and having dropped "Colored" from its name and added "Incorporated," the federation is consumed with restoring the Jackson-Community House, a property on city, state, and national registries of historic places. In 1943, President Zenobia Johnson, an Anna M. Duncan member, led the federation in purchasing this two-story, antebellum Union Street edifice, which was home to U.S. Attorney Jefferson Franklin Jackson, who built it. Known as the Jackson House for ninety years, black women rechristened it "The Community House." In the era of legal segregation and discrimination, with its relative scarcity of public funds and services in African American areas, the house proved invaluable. Notably, it functioned as a Girl Scouts headquarters, a popular and wholesome teenage rendezvous, an adult social and civic center, the regular meeting site of the Women's Political Council, and beginning in December 1948, the city's first public library for blacks. In time the building housed Consuelo Harper's kindergarten, which became the first program in her now thriving Central Alabama Opportunities Industrialization Center (OIC). Also, the edifice has served as a venue for an unwed mothers' Stork's Nest, voter registration, youth leadership training, tutorial and counseling programs, civic meetings, family reunions, receptions, and weddings.

In retrospect, it might seem that I was destined to become involved in the Montgomery City Federation of Women's Clubs, Inc., as well as the Anna M. Duncan Club and the St. John's Working Club, because they represent constructive continuity with the past. This quality is appealing to a historian who grew up in Daytona Beach, Florida, a tourist city incorporated in the 1870s, and thus lacking an antebellum past. This absence, when combined with a relatively small black population in the early decades, has in part caused the demise of traditions in the black community that extend back to the early twentieth century. The Silver Leaf Charity Club, Daytona's last historic black women's federated unit, for example, passed into extinction in 1995 after a protracted illness.

"Destined" or otherwise, I became affiliated with the Working Club in an unorthodox manner. In 1982, when I joined the St. John's AME Church, the authoritarian but wise pastor immediately announced, "I am assigning Mrs. Smith to the St. John's Working Club." While reared in AME and United Methodist traditions, I had never heard of a working club. Besides, no pastor had ever previously "assigned" anybody to this unit. Clubwomen either sought out new members or, less frequently, an individual joined because she had approached club members about entry. I didn't know what to think. My first meeting didn't help. The women, numbering about twenty, appeared to be a generation or two older than my thirty-something. I wondered if the pastor thought that I was a little old lady. The devotions were extended; the pace of the meeting was slow; membership was inexpensive; and if unable to attend a meeting, one had to report her excuse to a contact person, who in turn relayed it to the body. These qualities evoked an earlier era instead of a with-it, contemporary tempo. But in short order I came to value what I had initially thought strange, especially since members welcomed me with open arms. Today I find attractive also the gradually achieved age range of active members, which extends from thirty-plus to ninety-eight.

Membership in the Working Club indirectly led to my entry into the Duncan Club. The short, matronly, and kindly Montgomery native Susie Knox McKissack, a quintessential little old lady who belonged to both organizations, would not be content unless I joined her civic association. In one sense I felt a bit more comfortable in my initial meeting of the Duncan Club than I had in the Working Club because out of almost twenty women, several my own age greeted me. A few of the same individuals belonged to both groups. Another similarity was that Duncan members usually held regular meetings in their homes and always served dinner. Getting to know like-minded women from all over town as we broke bread together enticed me. While always assuming my financial responsibilities, I could take or leave the club business. By arriving late, but in time for dinner, too often it was the latter. That is until May 2000, when I was elected the twenty-fourth Duncan Club president.

While serving as head of the venerable Anna M. Duncan Club, an affiliate of the Montgomery City Federation, of necessity I became involved in federation business. Also propelling me toward that end was my election—a fait accompli without my knowledge—as federation historian in 2000. Attending my first meeting after these new responsibilities, I realized how writer Jessie Fauset felt seventy-eight years earlier, when she witnessed in 1922 her first convention of the National Association of Colored Women. In the *Crisis* magazine she disclosed, "It has its faults. . . . I saw too much bickering, too many personal, petty, needless jealousies, too many antagonisms insufficiently veiled, not enough appreciation of the fact that one person or one club or one faction cannot have all the honor." While Fauset concluded, "But with all this, there was much more to encourage and inspire" (260), I am just arriving at that point regarding the federation. It must standardize operating procedures, a process partially under way in the form of a revised voting process for officers, based upon the number of members in each club. And, like its constituent units, the federation must offer more services, in addition to the meritorious and challenging work of restoring the Jackson-Community House under the capable direction of project manager

Sangernetta Gilbert Bush. Once operations are centered in the restored headquarters building, members anticipate that the federation will do this.

Service is what the Duncan Club and the St. John's Working Club are about. In the early 1990s, Albertine Moore Campbell, who had then been in both organizations for sixty years, glowingly recalled highlights of their service. Relative to the Duncan Club, she spoke of sponsorship of a youth club, an annual nursing scholarship, supplies and services to the Father Purcell Memorial Center for Exceptional Children, the same for the Mt. Meigs youth facility, and furniture and accessories for the reception room of Community House. While hanging on to most traditional commitments, currently the club also contributes $100 annually to the Cleveland Avenue YMCA; gives a Mother's Day Program and gifts to patrons in a senior health-care facility; ushers for the Frederick Douglass Hall Community Choir; and sponsors an African American Women's Forum. In 2002, the organization launched the Anna M. Duncan Youth Cultural Club, which wowed a large audience at the state convention in Montgomery with poems from James Weldon Johnson's *God's Trombones*.

Regarding St. John's Working Club, Campbell characterized it as a "grand heritage" for the St. John's Church family. The essence of that heritage beckons one and all to greater faithfulness in "little" deeds of kindness and love. In an interview with me in April 1985, as the club historian, Campbell related that most of its history centered in raising money for the church, with activities ranging from selling club-made quilts to sponsoring teas and flea markets. All that is history, however. Today the club's most visible projects are the annual award of a $1,000 scholarship to a high school senior, made possible in part by endowments from two deceased members; and decorating the church for Christmas, the results of which one bishop likened to a Christmas card. Even with these activities, the organization continues traditional giving to help finance specific church projects, assists with church dinners on special occasions, donates to food and clothes closets, and checks monthly on sick and confined members of the congregation.

The Working Club, Duncan Club, and Montgomery City Federation have been blessed by ASU. They benefit from its facilities and human resources. Early in the twentieth century, St. John's Working Club sold food and craft goods at then fashionable lawn parties sponsored by its church, held on ASU ground now occupied by Tullibody Hall. In my own time but still years ago, a federation fund-raiser took place at the university. In January 2002 the Duncan Club held its African American Women's Health Forum in ASU's Alabama Room. But more important than facilities are the ASU graduates, faculty, and staff who constitute a large percentage of each of my womanist groups. About fifty percent of the twenty-two members in my church auxiliary are either ASU grads or faculty, and sometimes both. In 2001 all three of my organizations were led by ASU devotees—two were graduates and one, yours truly, was a faculty member. Today, the Duncan Club and Working Club still claim ASU women as leaders. Having served a two-year term as head of the former, I am now the president of the latter.

Albertine Campbell, who died in 1994, personified the close relationship between university and community, of which my clubs are a part. Her family came with the school when it moved to Montgomery from Marion, Alabama, about a century ago, because her father taught at the school. With the exception of her college years at Fisk University, Campbell lived almost all her life on Jackson Street, across from the campus. She was married for more than fifty years to ASU's Superintendent of Buildings and Grounds. Like Campbell's family, my family moved to Montgomery because of work at ASU. This made me available for local voluntary associations. Without ASU, all my womanist circles would be poorer in material resources, in an educated rank and file, and in leadership. I am pleased with the historic and current ties between the university and them.

Also, I am pleased to have contributed to womanist causes. Yet, I have gained more from the St. John's Working Club and the Anna M. Duncan Club than I've given. The older women have at times mentored me in protocol, graciousness, and faithfulness; the younger ones have encouraged me with their energy, initiative, and creativity. I have profited much from the speakers and roundtables that often characterize their monthly programs. The clubs have given me a greater sense of place and belonging. They have supported me as I have encountered the vicissitudes of life. In other words, I've found rewarding sisterhoods.

Novelist Sue Monk Kidd explains underlying premises of such fellowships. "When women bond together in a community in such a way that 'sisterhood' is created, it gives them an accepting and intimate forum to tell their stories and have them heard and validated by others. The community not only helps to heal their circumstance, but encourages them to grow into their destiny" (8).

I believe that Montgomery and cities like it will always need grassroots womanist units working within larger contexts to enhance educational, social, and cultural opportunities. In them, progressive women will almost inevitably obtain a larger understanding and appreciation of their strength, race pride, and community. If current clubs falter, new ones will replace them—although they will lack the rich and cherished heritage our foremothers have bequeathed. I sense that in Montgomery I am a link in a long line of civic and spiritually minded black women. Here, I am living a womanist legacy.

6 / I Pledge Allegiance to
My "Black-Eyed Susan" University

Annie P. Markham

In the fall of 1987, my husband and I moved with our children to Montgomery, Alabama, to work at Alabama State University. In moving from Jackson, Mississippi, I left behind what I had considered a utopia: we were surrounded by family and friends, had a good working environment, and were actively involved in church and in the community. I had worked toward being a self-fulfilling, reproducing woman, rearing a family, belonging to myriad social clubs, and indulging in all my creativeness. After an enriching thirteen-year experience teaching at a community college, it would be a challenge for me to adjust to teaching at a historically black university, even though I had graduated from one myself. It only added to my ambivalence that my husband was named the head football coach at ASU, because I knew how inimical many people are to newcomers, especially coaches. Once the die was cast, however, there was no turning back. In less than a month, we packed our bags and moved to Montgomery, home of the mighty ASU Hornets.

It was at that time that I pledged to make ASU my "black-eyed Susan" school. I first heard that term used by Dr. Margaret Walker Alexander, often described as "the most famous author nobody knows." A twentieth-century voice from the South, she worked at a historically black college and university for thirty years, and was first exposed to black campus life by her parents, who had taught for twenty years at HBCUs themselves. Her most popular works include *Jubilee* and "For My People." Dr. Walker, as she was called, taught African American literature and creative writing at six colleges and universities, three white and three black, but affectionately used the term "black-eyed Susan" when referring to my alma mater, Jackson State University, where she worked the longest, and where there is now a research center for the study of the twentieth-century African American named in her honor.

Coming to teach at ASU was my chance to discover exactly what Dr. Walker meant by a "black-eyed Susan" school and to join her in pledging my allegiance. There are many similarities between the black-eyed Susan flower and historically black colleges and universities, beginning with fortitude and resiliency. The black-eyed Susan stands tall on hairy stems that make it difficult for insects to climb and devour, while HBCUs stand erect on traditions of self-determination and hard work that make them thrive. The black-eyed Susan thrives even in poor soil, requiring very little attention, while HBCUs continue to survive limited financial appropriations and social neglect, providing fellowship in a collective experience. The flower often grows in adverse conditions but always stands stately. Many HBCUs have stood proudly in the face of adverse circumstances, as ASU has done for over 135 years.

Alabama State University especially resembles the black-eyed Susan because it shares the same colors—black and gold. The flower's petals of gold, surrounding a huge black eye, are symbolic of ASU, surrounded by people of all nationalities in its endeavor to provide equal opportunities for all. The huge black eye in the center of the flower represents the heart of the university, the men and women attending and working to make dreams become reality and being a beacon in the community. While the black-eyed Susan provides rich nectar for butterflies, ASU provides a rich education accessible to all who seek it. Alike in so many ways, both hold out the promise of a bright future.

Keeping these similarities in mind was a help to me when I arrived at ASU because, at the time, my problems seemed manifold. I had to meet many new people, become familiar with different administrators, adjust to a different environment, keep my family together on a personal level, work with students on a professional level, and continue to work for human causes on a national level. From the moment my husband accepted the head coaching position, I knew I had to have the dexterity of a juggler. I immediately became surrogate mother to the many athletes under his supervision, and my allegiance to the athletic program was nonpareil. Along with the other coaches' wives, I attended both in-town and out-of-town football games, hosted and attended many social functions, and was a number one cheerleader. I became totally immersed in my black-eyed Susan school, in academics as well as in athletics.

One of the most fulfilling ways I have been able to demonstrate my allegiance has been by working with the Campus Outreach Ministry, sponsored at that time by churches of various denominations in Birmingham, Alabama. I first became involved because two of my former students had gone on to receive religious training, and I was one of their financial supporters. Since my church, Hutchinson Street Missionary Baptist Church, was selected as their "home site" in Mongomery, I was a logical person to invite to join with them in their ministry. We hired three young people (two males and one female) full-time to do spiritual work on the ASU campus, focusing especially on the dormitories. Although these missionaries had trained for many years, they had to spend at least one additional summer in intense training in Panama City, Florida, before they could begin this particular mission. For two years, from 1995 to 1996, they ministered to students and others on campus, under the auspices of the minister at the home site. The missionaries were creative in showing Christian students alternative outlets. For example, there would be wholesome dinner engagements, outings at parks, field trips, and weekly Bible study sessions. One inspiring workshop for the young women was presented at Mt. Zion AME Zion Church by Reverend Cecelia Williams-Bryant, who spoke on exploring spiritual disciplines. Another outing was held in Birmingham for a weekend where several male and female facilitators presented workshops on living a wholesome life the Christian way. As one of the sponsors, I was at the weekly Bible study with students and facilitators, and I attended most other engagements. I supervised one of the leaders, who created a newsletter to keep us apprised of our accomplishments, and we were blessed tremendously by our efforts.

Realizing that the best way for me to serve my black-eyed Susan school was to challenge students and to heighten their social consciousness, I still had to find ways to provide opportunities for them to effect change. Having been assigned a new course, Humanities 103—Humanities through the African American Experience—I had to decide how to get my students motivated and concerned about the needs and desires of others in the surrounding community.

Little did I know that divine providence would intervene and that my church home would provide the serendipitous link between classroom and society. During the fall of 1989, my church joined with sister churches in Montgomery, black and white, to serve the needs of the residents in Montgomery's nine public housing communities and public schools. The Montgomery STEP Foundation (Strategies to Elevate People) includes twenty-seven churches from ten denominations. Some of the ministries available are tutoring and mentoring in churches each week, evangelism and discipleship programs in all housing communities, and Drug Free Clubs. Certain components of the STEP program are federally funded, and the program received the recognition as one of the top organizations in the country by the U.S. Department of Housing and Urban Development in 1999. Hutchinson Missionary Baptist Church, just three blocks from the ASU campus, sponsors the program locally, providing transportation for the students, purchasing school supplies, purchasing weekly refreshments, purchasing Christmas gifts, and providing gifts to reward honor students or other deserving students.

I have found that my black-eyed Susan university is blessed to have students willing to give of themselves by sharing in such missions in their community and in other ventures throughout the United States. With just a little encouragement, ASU students utilize their skills, talents, and abilities as they pursue meaningful careers, lifelong learning, and service to others. I am the liaison person between ASU students and Hutchinson Street Baptist Church and, in spite of the many responsibilities in and out of school, became the director in 1992 and am currently serving in that capacity. The overall mission of the program is to provide, via tutoring and mentoring, an environment and set of experiences wherein young children from nearby Tulane Court Housing Project can grow and live satisfying and meaningful lives. With the help of ASU student volunteers, we tutor and teach children to apply spiritual principles to their relationships with their families, with other individuals of different sexes, ages, and racial and ethnic backgrounds, and with their communities. We have been able to assist many young people from the lower echelon of society in becoming academically sound. Of the twenty-five youngsters we started with this school term, at least half have made the "A-B" Honor Roll each grading period. By providing prizes and recognizing those who excel academically, we motivate our youngsters to succeed. Also, by taking them on educational tours, such as museums and movies, we are able to help them become socially adjusted.

How do ASU students know about the STEP program? At the beginning of each semester, I write the word "synergism" on the board. We discuss the meaning—that when two join to produce more than they total (when one plus one makes three) we have synergism. Then I ask interested persons to work with me in a synergistic project, so we can make a difference in somebody's life. Attempting to make my Humanities class a service-learning class, I apprise them of various capacities in which they may serve: as tutors, mentors, anger management facilitators, Bible storytellers, music leaders, etc. I challenge those students without jobs or Wednesday evening classes (the tutoring days) to assist. Understanding the importance of being involved, students come and many recruit their friends. Some students play musical instruments, some tell Bible stories, some sing, some tutor, but all serve. Our reservoir of student volunteers is inexhaustible. As with all things, some students are more committed than others, but many ASU students work in the program their entire college career, others for a semester, and some just a couple of times. When the student volunteers keep in touch with the youngsters and their parents through the week, the youngsters tend to perform better and make the honor roll. One of our former participants is doing very well at the Booker T. Washington Magnet High School. One is reigning as "Queen" of Houston Hills Jr. High School this year, and one of our young male participants was captain of his senior high football team. Four of the young people have even joined our church and are in our youth choir. Almost all of our former participants whom I could locate have finished high school and entered college.

Amazed and encouraged by what ASU student volunteers were able to accomplish, I have gone on to develop an alternative pedagogy specifically designed to effect change in the community. This strategy has students read, witness, research, and serve. At the beginning of one semester, I assigned students *Rosa Lee* by Leon Dash. This work addresses many social issues plaguing society, such as violence against women, rape, and drug abuse. After spirited discussions of the work in class, students watched the documentary, witnessing firsthand some of the problems of the underclass; then students researched at least one of the issues addressed in their community or in their college community and wrote about their chosen topic. They examined the many forces which brought Rosa Lee to her unfortunate condition. They examined the roles of the family, community, church, school, and the welfare system. A final component of their assignment was to decide the best way for society to serve people in similar situations in their own community or in neighboring communities. Just as the worst team in the NBA has permission to draft the best player in order to strengthen the weakest link, students had to suggest ways to strengthen the weakest link in the community.

A reading that was custom-made for the kind of learning that took place for several semesters in Humanities 103 was yet to come. During the 1994 school year, I assigned students *The Economic Emancipation of African Americans,* by Richard Barber Sr. After much spirited dialogue about this book in class, students had to decide the best way to serve their fellow man. Impressed with the community service Mr. Barber had been motivated to do with a penny long before Oprah Winfrey and others, both locally and nationally, caught on to this "penny project," students agreed to donate, find, or solicit a minimum of five pounds of pennies, or five dollars. Their motto was: "A little becomes a lot when a lot give a little." They raised over 40,000 pennies for humanity, working harmoniously toward a goal. Euphoria spilled over from each one to the other, especially as they used their majors to serve in a particular area. For example, the English and speech majors spearheaded the letter writing, the business majors took charge of the financing, and the communications majors took care of the publicity. Every student in the class participated in some manner. We met several times after school hours, even on Sundays, but they did not mind. Once they collected the pennies, they voted to attack the alarming rates of illiteracy by purchasing reading materials for an elementary school.

Students also decided that they would involve a black-owned bookstore in the project in order to show support for black enterprises. They had discussed Booker T. Washington's phrase, "No people ever got upon its feet and obtained the respect and confidence of the world . . . without a solid economic foundation" (Delmarva Business League). Now it was time for students to network, after hours, to bring the project to a successful conclusion.

One group met to decide the types of books to recommend, and the grade levels and school to target; another group was responsible for purchasing the books at Roots and Wings, a local black-owned bookstore they had identified. Though the project had grown to involve a great deal of out-of-class work, I heard not one complaint because the students were working toward goals to which they were fully committed. Many admitted that they had never been to the bookstore before, but said they would return. They had become adamant about doing business with minority business owners because Mr. Barber's book stresses that the way out of poverty for blacks is through economic empowerment.

After two months of hard work, the group that had done the research to see which schools needed the books because they did not have a federal grant decided on the target school, Lovelace Elementary School. We met the night before presenting the books to autograph them. The students liked the idea of having their names, along with their university's name, on the inside of the books they presented. In their own way, they would be a part of history with their names written in books that would be read by many classes to come.

The mission was accomplished. Students proudly presented the books to the librarian and the students at Lovelace Elementary School. Nothing could have pleased them more than to have the media present also and to see themselves in the paper the next day. With the help of faculty, other students, parents, and local businesses, students in Humanities 103 had made an impact on the community. A few individuals emerged remarkably well versed in works by and about African Americans and the class as a whole experienced a remarkable growth. All had gained fresh perspectives on ways to emancipate African Americans. Most importantly, they had learned the value of synergism.

To this day I am in contact with many of my former students, including those who participated in the Campus Outreach Ministry program. And I continue today to do whatever I can to benefit the students of ASU, who come to this school in ever-increasing numbers. I have served on many faculty committees, including the Lyceum Committee, which invites distinguished guests to campus to perform or lecture, and I have served as faculty chaperone for students presenting papers or performing skits at Southern Regional Honors Conference meetings throughout the South. Both on campus and off, I have served as surrogate mother, advisor, coach, chaperone, tutor, counselor, or friend, as needed. Taking to heart Booker T. Washington's statement, "Those who are happiest are those who do the most for others" (Washington 685), I have wished to serve, and to honor my pledge of allegiance to ASU, my black-eyed Susan school.

Black life in Montgomery centered on Alabama State College, particularly for children who grew up on the campus. In the basement of the school's science building, Beverly Hall, Wiletta McGinty presided over the nursery-kindergarten. In the 1945 graduating class were, first row from left, Jean Smith, Peggy Ann Taylor, Rosalyn Oliver, Kathy Dunn, Paris Frasier, Ann Patricia Herring; back row from left, Carver Green, Dorothy Ann Duncan, Sangernetta Gilbert, Alberta Anderson, Harold Gamble, and Willie Ward. *Photo courtesy of Kathy Dunn Jackson.*

In his long career at Alabama State, C. Johnson Dunn (1901–1988) served as dean of students, athletic director, basketball coach, and economics teacher. He came to the institution at the request of President H. Councill Trenholm, his schoolmate at Atlanta's Morehouse College. After marrying G. Faustine Hamblin, he took up residence across the street from the Trenholms. A member of Dexter Avenue Baptist Church, in 1955–56 Dunn frequently transported bus boycotters in his automobile. *Photo courtesy of Kathy Dunn Jackson.*

G. Faustine Hamblin Dunn (1904–1988) came to Montgomery in 1911 when her father became pastor of the city's earliest black church, the Old Ship AME Zion, founded in 1852. After receiving a bachelor's degree from Livingstone College in Salisbury, North Carolina, she taught Latin and social studies and worked as the guidance counselor at the secondary school of Alabama State College. Dunn joined other women professionals at the college in the Women's Political Council, the local civic group that launched the Montgomery Bus Boycott. *Photo courtesy of Kathy Dunn Jackson.*

In the early 1950s under the direction of assistant basketball coach Doc Crawford, junior high girls from the secondary school of Alabama State College rooted for the college basketball team. Shown here, from left to right, Sylvia Motley, Johnelia Hardy, Peggy Ann Taylor, Carmen Prindle, Kathy Dunn, Laurel Anderson, and Dorothy Ann Duncan. *Photo courtesy of Kathy Dunn Jackson.*

Kathy Dunn, escorted by Troy Story Jr., is introduced to society at the 1958 Emanon Club's annual Debutante Ball, held at the college's Lockhart Gymnasium. *Photo courtesy of Kathy Dunn Jackson.*

Tullibody Hall was constructed in 1906 to replace the original frame building with the same name at Montgomery's black state school. In the 1950s, the second floor housed the college auditorium. The ground and first floors were the home of the Laboratory High School, grades seven through twelve, for which a waiting list always existed. Lab High maintained small classes, strict rules, and high standards. The school closed in 1971, and the building was razed. Today, Tullibody Hall for the arts stands on the site. *Photo courtesy of Alabama State University Special Collections.*

For more than thirty years, President H. Councill Trenholm provided leadership to Alabama State College, walking a tightrope between repressive white control of the institution and faculty and student desire for liberation. In 1962 controlling whites forced him into retirement. Dressed here for his August 1950 silver anniversary at the college, Trenholm stands with his young son Harper, and, left to right, his wife Portia, and daughters Edwina and Portia Yvonne. *Photo courtesy of Kathy Dunn Jackson.*

PART THREE

Non-Southern
What Difference?

7 / Portrait of the Artist as a Young White Man

Robert Ely

To the best of my knowledge, there were no African Americans living in DeKalb County, Indiana, when I was a boy growing up on the farm in the 1950s and '60s. We lived about a mile from a small town of perhaps a thousand citizens. There were a few streets of dilapidated shacks, owned or rented by poor whites, which everyone referred to as "Niggertown." There were "sundown laws" that prevented African Americans from remaining in the small rural villages between the hours of sundown and sunrise. It was well known by everyone that the philanthropist who built the public park in a neighboring town (and named it after himself) had put a restrictive covenant in the deed which specified that the park would be removed and the land would revert to his heirs in the event that any African American should ever choose to live within the sanctified, white city limits.

So much for racism as something peculiar to the southern states. It was, and it remains, as much at home amid the cornfields of the Midwest as it ever was in the cotton fields of the South. What makes the racism I grew up with so heinous in retrospect, and so different, is that no one even *knew* any black people. They only knew that they feared and hated "them" in the abstract, and I think that this abstract fear and hatred are what Hannah Arendt had in mind in her famous phrase "the banality of evil."

I did not embrace this state of affairs, nor did I rebel against it. It was just "the way things *were*," as so many have said, from sea to shining sea.

Yet change was definitely blowin' in the wind. Black-and-white TV newsreel footage of Bull Connors raging, of vicious police dogs attacking children, and of water cannons turned upon innocent protestors are all engraved in my memory like gouged steel. So are the images of thousands of black Americans marching up Dexter Avenue toward the old capitol in Montgomery after the long trek from Selma.

What was going on, anyway? The only person I actually recalled as a "Negro" was a kind man who had untangled my fishing line from some brush near his boat as Dad and I cast for bream from the river bank when I was twelve. I waved "thanks," and the gentleman tipped his hat to us. Who were all these other "Negroes" on TV? I had a map puzzle of the United States as a child, and I could easily point to Alabama, name its capital city, its major commodities, and its surrounding states. But where was it *really*?

For my father (a World War II vet who had traveled the world and found little to his liking), the Klan "had the right idea," and whites who lived south of our own county line were "hillbillies." (Indeed, some who lived north of us were "hillbillies" too, in his judgment.) Dad really didn't discriminate. He was deeply prejudiced, frightened, and hateful of *any* race, religion, nationality, region, or hairstyle not known on our small farm. In short, he was an angry man and a bully, and he died of his anger at a young age. As for learning about Alabama and its rich mixture of people, well, we once traveled as far south as Nashville, Tennessee, but Dad didn't like it, and we left quickly.

Sometimes, for "amusement," the older, meaner boys at my country school would cruise to industrial Fort Wayne in neighboring Allen County. There, they would drive down Hannah Street, in the black district, with whiffle bats. They would stop at street corners where they summoned young black boys, and sometimes men, to their car windows, and then whacked 'em upside the head with their bats and sped off, squealing their tires.

Truthfully, I never did this. I never even came close. I did not associate with that kind of crowd. I was clean-cut and decent. Mama made sure of that. I got good grades and drove the Homecoming Queen (white, naturally) on the back of a convertible (also white) in the parade.

Funny, though, how "what goes around comes around," as they say. A couple of years after the assassination of Dr. Martin Luther King Jr., I was peacefully walking in the lobby of my college dormitory, minding my own business, when I was suddenly and for no reason at all viciously clobbered in the face by an angry young black student, recently recruited by my pacifist church college from (of course) Fort Wayne. I think the young man was drunk, but that is not the point.

I did not turn the other cheek, nor did I run away or strike back. I was too stunned. There were abundant witnesses in the lobby, and the young man was given a hearing and suspended from the college for a while. This was in 1970, and I continued to adhere to my "liberal" views about race, class, the war, materialism, and nonviolence—views for which I had marched, carried candles, and been tear-gassed by the National Guard.

Or did I? Did I "continue to adhere" to my "liberal" views? Indeed, did I ever really hold them in the first place? Or was it just the fashion? I have no idea, but time would offer further challenges for me, just as it does continually for all of us, black, white, or other.

I graduated from Manchester College in Indiana, worked two years in advertising, and hated every minute of it. I felt I had "sold out," and so I returned to higher education, earned my MA and very nearly completed a PhD in English and philosophy at Purdue University. I achieved perfect marks throughout my graduate study, and I had published some reputable scholarly articles. But, by 1977, I found myself "burned out" with graduate school and the menial wages of a teaching assistant. I wanted to pay off my debts, have an income like other people my age, and finish my PhD sometime down the road. I desperately wanted to teach full-time. I believed in the power of education to change people's lives and to make the world a better place.

This was at a time when full-fledged PhDs in English (my primary field) were standing in line to get jobs as taxi drivers. But I was determined. I knew I was a good teacher with certain gifts and experience not possessed by others. So I applied diligently for any and all college teaching positions I could find. I wrote well over two hundred letters of application, and I had some interviews. A couple of them produced job offers that I turned down.

Then, in the summer of 1977, I saw an ad for a teaching position in English at Alabama State University in Montgomery. The ad made it clear that ASU was a historically black university, and, I must admit, that fact gave me pause. I knew immediately that I was being tested. I was "a liberal." I was not "a racist." I believed in "the equality of all human beings without regard to race, creed, or color," and I had stood up and defended those views in the face of some serious opposition from others. But was this the sort of job I wanted? Was I ready for a genuine, personal, public, professional commitment to a black institution? I had always imagined myself teaching in a small, largely (though not totally) white liberal arts college with a group of good, like-minded, "liberal" colleagues and students.

Thus, I had reservations. The South had always been attractive to me. But "historically black"? I wasn't sure. Would I "fit in"? Would I be embraced, merely tolerated, or despised for my own color? Would I be accepted by my white neighbors? By my own father? Would the university be "academic enough" for me? In short, would ASU be "good enough for me"? And did I really want to be "in the minority"? I was not proud of those questions then, and I do not admit to them proudly now. It is just "the way things *were*" with me. Was I up to the test that looked me in the face when I read the ad about teaching at ASU? Did I have enough faith in my own convictions to act upon them and apply for the job? I was not frightened by the idea, but I was thoughtful. There was a deadline for applications, and I knew I had to choose, just as we all must choose, each moment of our lives.

It was absolutely clear to me that my beliefs were no better than my willingness to act upon them. So I put my best paper in my typewriter and wrote the most eloquent and appealing job application letter I knew how to write. I wrote with the same conviction and persuasiveness I would have used had I been applying to teach at Harvard or any other college or university. I wanted the job, and I knew I had to be true to myself.

Yes, I wrote the letter and applied for the job offered at Alabama State University. Yes, I was blessed to have an interview and the kindest, most cordial reception anyone could receive anywhere. Yes, I was offered the job, and yes, I happily took it.

As I look back over half a lifetime, at nearly a quarter of a century of teaching at ASU, I see very clearly how that simple decision "has made all the difference," as Robert Frost put it (131). Of course, there are other roads I could have taken. There are other experiences and rewards I would have enjoyed. I suspect many directions would have proven interesting. But I am absolutely convinced that there is no road I could have chosen which would have led to a deeper, richer, or more satisfying and rewarding life than that which I have enjoyed as a citizen of Montgomery and a faculty member at Alabama State University.

It is reasonable to ask how I can make such a grand statement and make it with such conviction. Human personality is multifaceted, and our experience of life is multilayered. Thus, any answer I offer to this question (from the most simple to the most complex) is likely to be partial, sketchy, inconclusive, and possibly unconvincing. This is particularly true in light of the fact that, like most academics, I am a perfectionist, inclined to believe I am uniquely tuned in to the "really right answer," skeptical of others' conclusions, and, often, downright cynical. In other words, I have complained as loudly and bitterly as anyone about various academic policies and procedures which have been debated, adopted, and pursued by ASU over the years, and I will no doubt continue to do so.

How, then, can I claim with a straight face that my experience at the University has been so very deep, rich, and satisfying?

One easy answer is "the people." I have been blessed to work beside other teachers and administrators whose intelligence, competence, dedication, kindness, humanity, and capacity for love are unsurpassed in my experience. I have disagreed and even fought with them from time to time, for no human organization whatever—whether the Democrats, the Republicans, or the Screen Actors' Guild—is more contentious, difficult, and ego-driven than a university faculty and administration. More often, however, we have worked diligently together toward common goals derived from rational debate, our collective experience, goodwill, and commitment to a better world. I have loved my colleagues, and I know that they have loved me. I have learned far more from them than I could ever hope to teach, and for all of these blessings, I am deeply grateful.

But, in fact, the answer, "the people," is altogether too easy. There are fine people and miserable people wherever one goes. And academics, wherever one goes, are always among the most interesting people, even when one finds them on their worst behavior. In other words, there are fine, dedicated, and highly interesting people at other colleges and universities besides Alabama State University.

An equally easy, but also unsatisfactory, answer is "our success stories." I have always believed that the frontier of American democracy in our time is the front edge of my desk. The countless physicians, attorneys, engineers, teachers—highly functional and contributing citizens of so many professions—who have graduated from ASU and traversed that border successfully have indeed warmed my heart. Often, it seems, the harvest of the teaching profession is not properly measured until many years have passed. I have had innumerable former students, successful in their twenties and thirties, flag me down in supermarkets, malls, and parking lots with, "Hey, Mr. Ely! Are you still at ASU? I'll never forget your class. You were tough, but you were fair. You really taught me a lot!" Or words to that effect.

But, once again, that answer is too easy. Teaching will always produce its successes and its failures. It is not just "the people," whether colleagues or students, that have made ASU especially rewarding to me. Nor is it the rich history of the institution and its general significance in American life, as much as those factors might mean to me as well.

Somehow, my experience goes deeper. Deeper even than my gratitude for the respect I have received at the University and the genuine, concerned supportiveness I have felt there in pursuing my own academic, personal, and spiritual growth.

So, what *is* it then, this "deep" thing?

Nothing worthwhile is ever simple. Perhaps the unique contribution of Alabama State University to my life is that it has allowed me to be lost and found at the same time. Such a statement might sound like a contradiction, an absurd impossibility, or a conundrum at best, but it is not. It is a condition I believe African Americans understand very well. In other words, I have been blessed to share, to some degree, in the African American experience of ambiguity. Often viewed as an alien by my white acquaintances and neighbors, I am also (inevitably, I think) a bit of an alien on campus. As the great spiritual puts it, I too have sometimes felt "like a motherless child."

But it is not a bad thing at all, this being lost and found at the same time. In my experience, an appreciation and a welcoming of ambiguity make our lives richer and our souls more human. Thus, I have been lost in wonder at the beauty of life and the enduring capacity of individuals to rise above their situations and become more than they are. I have been found as well, in learning that my life can make a difference and that I can, in fact, contribute in many ways uniquely my own.

Occasionally shunned by some, I have had the pleasure to live and work in a city, state, and region that I love deeply and where I have been deeply loved, accepted, and appreciated by many friends of all races and at all levels of society. Alabama State University has allowed me to pursue my life with dignity, purpose, and meaning. I have been more than a visitor here. I have lived my own journey. I have contributed work of quality and integrity, and that knowledge goes deep in me and gives me peace.

I got off the bus in Montgomery and happily forgot to get back on again. In return, I have received nothing less than the freedom to go my own way.

And what more could anyone desire?

8 / City on a Hill

Karl E. Westhauser

Historians try to be objective. That means that when I tell a story I'm supposed to shine a light on the facts while doing my best to hide out in the shadows, as if the story were telling itself without me. But I found a light already shining when I got here, and it's been changing the way I see things. That's the story I want to tell. For a change, I'm really just a witness.

~

There's plenty of history here, of course, but it wasn't history that got me hooked on this place at the start. It was talking with a secretary when I applied for a job. The voice that answered the telephone gave meaning to the phrase "bursting with good humor," and it glowed with warmth and good will. To me this one woman was the voice of Alabama State University, plus the entire city of Montgomery, the whole state of Alabama, maybe even the South itself, all wrapped up together. The funny thing is that, like me, she isn't from around here at all. It turns out she's from Chicago. They come from everywhere, the people who call this place home, and they can make others feel at home here, too. I like knowing that most people I'll meet are not so consumed by worry for tomorrow, or anger about the past, that they can't make time for one another in the moment. It's a nice change from just about everywhere I have ever lived.

I share a lot of values with the people I meet here, and that's important to me. As in my native New York, people here look to the future—eyes on the prize. To me, the future matters a whole lot more than the past anyway, and change is the name of the game. Change may not happen fast here—not much does—but it's what's on people's minds. You can hear it in this motto from a student club I've served on campus: "What determines our future is not what is before us, nor what is behind us, but what is within us." I like to believe that, and being with others who do helps me feel that my optimism about the future might be justified. I find it easier to hope that all may yet be revealed, which is why I study history in the first place.

It's also why, every fall, I look forward to walking back into the classroom. Most eighteen-year-olds have not the slightest intention of taking history seriously, but the young people I meet know at least that history matters. That's because heritage matters here. Roots mean something to people. It seems everyone here, young or old, black or white, grew up knowing that much to be true. I know my students will finish my sentence for me when I say, "You can't know where you're going (if you don't know where you've been)." It means I have more common ground with the young people I teach here than I could expect at many other schools these days, and that gives me a lot to work with.

Not that I haven't had my doubts about the place. I didn't realize how deep my prejudices ran until I landed in Georgia and caught myself expecting to be picked up for talking funny by a fat, cigar-chewing, white sheriff, grinning from behind a dark pair of sunglasses. But whenever I'm in a new place, I'm all too aware of being different from everyone else, who all seem to me to be a lot alike. Down here, it seems everybody's family name is of English or Scots origin, and mine stands out. Few people are comfortable pronouncing my name for the first time, and frankly, some hardly seem to try. When one student mauled it more brutally than usual one year, her classmates surprised me by recognizing her mistake and actually chided her until she got it right!

At first I worried about just how much of a barrier my difference would be, and my experiences let me know it wasn't just a matter of getting over or glossing over my own preconceptions—my difference was real and my difference mattered. So I was, and still am, acutely aware that I am a Yankee in the South, a New York liberal in a conservative small town, an Ivy Leaguer on a SWAC campus—the list goes on and on. I used to be embarrassed by my difference but that's changed. Now I know better than ever who I am, and I'm more comfortable with myself. As a colleague of mine observed just the other day, over a fine southern lunch of fricasseed chicken and vegetables, you carry home with you wherever you go—and he's from a little place in rural Alabama called Pink's Bottom. For both of us, I know, home is something to be proud of and, even more, something to live up to. And when you know who you are and where you come from, you can better appraise your resources and put to good use whatever it is you find you have to offer.

It wasn't all that clear to me what I would have to offer when I started teaching here. But, when it comes to teaching, I'd have had a lot to figure out no matter where I was. That's because, like most college professors, I'd received no formal training in teaching—it's something you're expected to be bright enough to pick up along the way—and this was my first teaching job in any event. But people on this campus take teaching more seriously than most anyplace else, and they opened my eyes pretty quickly to lots of exciting possibilities. I remember the lightbulb switching on in my head during one seminar I attended about connections between writing and learning: I was asked to work out in my mind, and write down on paper, what goals I wanted my students to accomplish and what projects could be designed to help them do that. This may sound simple but it isn't, and it hadn't even crossed my mind. With lots of such support and encouragement from my colleagues, I've discovered an enthusiasm for teaching I never knew I had and like to think I can see in myself reflections of the professors I most admired when I was a student.

But a lot of people say black students need black role models in the classroom, and I can't be that. The closest I've come is being to one Honors student what she once called her "play-father," something I didn't understand until she graduated, when part of me was bursting with pride for his little girl and another part of me realized he was losing a daughter, and grieved. Early on, I'd actually made that bright young woman melt into tears in my office by marking up the first draft of her term paper with my usual enthusiasm, excited about the exceptional potential this first-semester freshman showed me and wanting to show her ways she could develop that potential. I forgot she wasn't used to that. She'd told me how she hated white people because, back up north where she came from, white teachers didn't care about black kids like her. She always demanded at least as much of me as I did of her, and I am grateful for those memories, which I might never have had at a white school.

I've found a niche for myself here. I take heart from the words of another of my colleagues, the descendant of a fine old Mississippi family that's given the world a well-known novelist, and at least one judge: she assures me that southerners don't hide their crazy people in the attic—they put them right out there on the front porch with the rest of the family. It makes me think fondly of southerners I'd met up north, some of whom qualify as some of the craziest people I ever knew, and as some of my favorite fellow creatures. Most of the time they'd leave me grinning like an idiot and trying to figure them out. Now, instead, I'm content to grin and let it go at that, because I'm beginning to be able to see myself, along with everyone else in the world, as crazy just like them. I've decided that I'd rather be with the rest of the family than all by myself, and if they can put up with me, then surely I can put up with them, too. I'm trying to become a more patient person, because someone who doesn't want others to rush to judgment about him shouldn't be too quick to judge, either. So, whenever I think someone is spouting off a lot of nonsense, I listen, try to smile, and remember I love them.

Like a lot of people, I've got some demons I'd like to get rid of. Yes, I'm a knee-jerk liberal, because as a child I was offended by the ignorant hatred and vicious stupidity that were all too apparent in the world. But I also realize how much hate and anger I wound up carrying around myself as a result and how much I'm stuck with even now, and I'm tired of it, finally. These days I like considering other ways of responding to the world, such as how the people of Birmingham reacted to the deaths of four little girls in the Ku Klux Klan bombing of the Sixteenth Street Baptist Church. One of their friends, now a colleague of mine, tells me blacks and whites still "spoke" when they passed each other on the street there, as they always had, and as everyone still does here. So I look forward, every spring, to teaching about Dr. King, and Gandhi, and the theory and practice of militant non-violence. I hope that one of these times I'll find it's changed something inside of me because, like my students, I have a lot of learning and growing yet to do. In the meantime, I must confess, I enjoy every opportunity to hold forth in self-righteous indignation, the time-honored privilege of the teaching historian.

I've learned a lot more about prayer, because there's so much of it around here. I can't say I have what's called a "church home," something many here think everyone should have. But some of the religious people here don't leave God behind when they step out in public, and often when I'm with them I feel we're not alone. Take the secretary who keeps her Bible on her desk and will help you know, if you spend some time with her, how good God is, or the imam of the local masjid, whose face shines with peace and goodwill. I haven't run into the sort of thing I used to hurry past, people screaming through their loudspeakers about Hell, or the white devils. Instead, I've had lots of welcome opportunities to hold hands in communion with students and colleagues, friends and strangers, and to listen to the University Choir— I really like the Choir—and to try lifting my own voice, such as it is. It's hard to escape the conclusion that the things I like about this place are extensions of the kind of faith so many people here seem to have, which is an awesome thing to contemplate. It's helped open up my heart in ways it hadn't known for a long time. I more cheerfully embrace the possibilities of each new day and more trustingly hope that, whatever trials may come in this life, I will have strength enough to face them.

People here must have a lot of strength, to judge by all they do—cheering the sick and staffing crisis lines, selling candy and running the Faculty-Staff Alliance, teaching Sunday school and getting out the vote. For many, the campus is an extension of the community and it certainly has been a starting point for me. As an advisor to a student organization, I lent a hand directing an after-school tutoring program down the street, and saw what a little extra attention can mean to a child. It affirmed the old liberal, Christian ideas that the world is what we make of it and that we can make a difference, but it was an eye-opener, too, seeing just how much remains to be done. I don't like encouraging those who would have us believe that a little charity makes up for failing so miserably to meet the needs of so many, but I see better now that each of us can choose to do something on our own. I also give something for student scholarships to the new University Trust fund every year. I like to think of it as investing in the future—our future—and helping some of my fellow citizens loosen up their own tight fists, since the state now has to match every gift with tax dollars, by court order.

The University itself is a monumental testament to what people can accomplish, and a well of inspiration. Take the story of how there came a time, back in the day, when the faculty's salaries could not be paid and they accepted food from the students' parents, and kept on teaching. I've never doubted the truth of that story, although the old gentleman who told it to me did like to have his fun, telling me to be sure to try the elephant ears at the state fair and not be squeamish—they're just *pigs'* ears, he said, and, with some mustard, not bad at all. I can hear him saying to himself: "Man, if he doesn't know it's fried dough with powdered sugar, he needs to get out there and learn something." All I know for sure is, that man taught history here for more years than I've been alive and kept on teaching history here until the day came when his students had to help him out of his classroom. Now it's up to the rest of us to remember and pass the stories along. But that's what history is, my own professors always said—not the deeds of kings but the doings of ordinary men and women, in all their ordinariness. It's important to me to believe that each life matters; and this place says it's so.

Few students come here knowing any more about this place than I did when I arrived, so it's a good thing for all of us that heritage is celebrated here. Throughout the year there are opportunities to participate in commemorative events such as Black History Month, the Martin Luther King Jr. Convocation, and Founder's Day. Over the years, we have heard, and even met, nationally prominent guest speakers few of us would have had much chance to see otherwise. At their best, events like these make us want to learn more and find ways of making our own contributions, as many student organizations do by paying tribute in song or dance and as this academic has done through research and writing. Soon after I got here I started looking further into the history of relations between blacks and whites, comparing what happened in colonial America with early developments in Europe, which is my area of special expertise, and ended up discovering things nobody knew before (Westhauser, 112–22). And that's what a university is supposed to be about, after all—people asking questions and looking for answers, making discoveries that change what is known. On the black campus, we all get to study the world from a changed perspective, no matter who we are, and each of us makes our own discoveries, big and small, every day.

Sad to say, many young people arrive here not even knowing that they have come to "the Birthplace of the Modern Civil Rights Movement." It was here that Rosa Parks refused to give up her seat on a city bus to a white man; her arrest that day triggered the boycott that galvanized black America and thrust the Reverend Martin Luther King Jr. upon the world stage. But it wasn't the civil rights movement that put this place on the map—nearly a hundred years earlier this place was the first capital of the Confederate States of America. From here was issued the order that began the Civil War, the telegram to South Carolina to fire upon Fort Sumter. The little red-brick church that invited the young King to come here to serve as its pastor stands just below the white-plastered form of the state capitol, sitting impressive upon a hill at the head of Dexter Avenue. At the top of its stone mountain of steps, Jefferson Davis stood to be sworn in as C.S.A. president. There, too, ended the four-days' march of those who set out from Selma on a quest for voting rights, sanctified by Bloody Sunday. At the bottom end of the short, sloping avenue is the square where slaves were bought and sold. There, Parks boarded her bus and sat down—directly across from the building, still standing, from which Davis's government sent its telegram.

It's a small town, in many ways, and a small world. Those few blocks downtown are now practically part of the neighborhood for me. I've paid bills and met friends for lunch there and, a couple of times, walked a little ways with those who, once a year (every year), retrace the entire length of the voting rights march like the stages of the cross. There's a profound intimacy about the place that you can't see in any photograph or find on any map. A lot seems to come together there and something greater seems to emerge. It may seem strange, but here I feel closer to my own hometown of New York City than I have ever felt anywhere else I have lived. It puts me in mind of other days gone by and my own past, growing up in the Catholicism my mother's grandparents brought over from Ireland and on dark brown cinnamon cookies "baked" for Christmas in a stove-top iron press, which my father's mother carried over from Germany. The families I remember achieved lives of quiet simplicity—and thought highly enough of their own ways to have little use for the ways of others. Yet I was always taught, as far back as I can remember, that I lived in the greatest city in the world, because its people came from everywhere and built something greater than themselves.

People sometimes like to say, with a trace of humor, "Here the past isn't dead—it isn't even past." But it can be too easy for me to think I know what they mean by that. One thing I discovered soon after coming here is that the Confederate battle flag *does not* fly from our capitol dome, a hot-button issue in other southern state capitals, nor was it incorporated into the state flag here during the civil rights movement as it was in other states of the old C.S.A. But a Confederate flag did fly from the dome one day, just a couple of years ago, after someone sneaked it up there in the dark of night. Greeted with some amusement was the news that a graying member of the state legislature was detained for clambering up there himself to remove the offensive symbol the next day! Forty years ago, that future legislator was a student here at the University, a history major, and one of those arrested for taking part in a sit-in at a whites-only lunch counter. He tells me he's been arrested in similar situations dozens of times since then, as most everyone here seems to know. He teaches a class here now, and has done so for thirty years. We share an office.

Times do change, of course, and change always brings new challenges. My office mate rose to the challenge of the brutal murder of an Alabama gay man by sponsoring legislation to expand the state's hate crimes provisions to include sexual orientation, and recently he derided the priorities of legislators proposing a state ban on gay marriage. I value the solidarity the old warrior stands for, and wonder what he would have made of another politically minded history major, a model young man who was one of my own students. On the morning after the 1994 election, this Honors freshman told the class that he had been working all semester as a volunteer in the governor's race and apologized for not being his usual self that day. Praising him for such mature public spirit and for having kept his grades up, too, I prepared to offer my condolences, knowing that the Democratic candidate favored on campus had lost. But it turned out that he had been partying all night, celebrating with the victor, a Republican who went on to slash funding for education, claim the Bill of Rights does not apply to the states, and ape a monkey on national television. I hope those unexpected developments gave him the shock of his young life. But I think of him all the more fondly because he surprised me a little, too, the political path he saw fit to venture upon a measure, in its own way, of how far we have come.

Fortunately, there are some things everyone still agrees on here, such as the importance of taking personal responsibility for what we do. It's a point my students will always make if I give them the chance. They say things like "Sweep off your own porch first," quoting their grandmothers. So it wouldn't be fair of me to act as if we don't understand each other, turning myself into one of those old timers that young people push out of the way, as happens a lot when times are changing. To be sure, there will be young people in every generation who will have trouble finding their way or figuring out the difference between getting a chance to succeed and getting a free ride. But here even *they* can learn better what's expected of them, which is one of the most important opportunities anyone could offer them. I have listened with interest to a balding alum, who was a protester back in his student days, tell an auditorium full of freshmen that they are in his house now and, if they don't like his rules, to go and get their own house. There's a kernel of truth there, I think, that all of us, of every generation, should be able to recognize and acknowledge, though each of us might express it differently. I would like to say that this is *our* house and that we must *all* treat everyone else with respect, because I, too, have come to call it home. And I, too, want us all to be proud of it.

~

In history, as in life, a lot depends on how you look at things and much of what you find depends on what you are looking for. If you wish to see it, you will find a great light shining here, as I have. For this historian, that light has illuminated the past as well as the present. Living in the city on a hill helps me to look to the future with renewed hope, and to try to do whatever needs doing along the way. "A city that is set on an hill cannot be hid. Neither do men light a candle and put it under a bushel, but on a candlestick; and it giveth light unto all that are in the house" (Matthew 5:14–15).

9 / Called Home

Margaret Holler Stephens

In the basement recreation hall of the church of my childhood hung a painting of Jesus with all of the children of the world gathered around him, a huge crowd of girls and boys in costumes from many lands. As a child, I grew up gazing at that painting and affirming its message: God is love, and Jesus loves all. In my child's wisdom, I adopted that credo for life. We also sang a song that set the painting's theme to words, and I sang that hymn loudly, joyfully, and in a child's clear, firm voice of faith and certainty. "Jesus loves the little children, all the children of the world; red or yellow, black or white, they are precious in his sight; Jesus loves the little children of the world."

Looking back, I sense that all of my life has been a journey and a preparation for teaching at Alabama State University, a historically black university that seeks to appreciate and uphold its diversity of race, gender, and ideas. I have come home to my earliest and deepest love, to a community of people who seek to be united in brotherhood, come home to my calling. When I arrived at Alabama State University in 1998, just blocks from the Montgomery church of Dr. Martin Luther King Jr., I found myself in the midst of a powerful legacy that continues to transform me. I find it difficult to express in words the initial, gradual, dawning sense of humility and awe I felt in response to this proud tradition, past and present. I found that the work begun by Dr. King and many before him is continuing at Alabama State University through the interactions of students, faculty, staff, and the surrounding community. Together we work toward Dr. King's dream and our dream: "the day when all of God's children" will experience equity and justice and the day when "we will be able to transform the jangling discords of our nation into a beautiful symphony of brotherhood" ("I Have a Dream" 86). I was introduced early in life to this fight for justice, for my paternal grandmother had suffered greatly in her native land due to ethnic hatred and oppression, and her sufferings had laid the brickwork of determination in my youthful personality. I willed that I would grow up to fight such prejudice and would help people gain their God-given rights in this often selfish and heartless world.

My grandmother, who came to live with us when I was a child, helped to raise me. A favorite childhood game for me and my friends playing on the black-and-white linoleum kitchen floor while my grandmother cooked and ironed was to crawl under her skirts and count the layers, for she seemed to wear most of the slips and skirts she owned. I wondered if she wore almost all of her clothes at once because she had been forced to leave her small white cottage in what is now Serbia with only the clothes on her back and a Bible in hand after World War II when Tito confiscated the homes, land, and possessions of people of German descent. Grandma Holler, though born and raised in Yugoslavia, was of German ancestry. Several generations earlier, Germans had been invited as a group to homestead and farm in then Austria-Hungary because of their industrious ways. A print of this historical migration now hangs on my bedroom wall. Because Nazi Germany had invaded Yugoslavia during the war, my grandmother and others like her had to pay, just as Japanese Americans suffered in our country during World War II. At about sixty-five years of age, my grandmother had walked out of her home at gunpoint (while my aunt and cousin hid in the cornstalks) and was compelled to live in a forced-labor camp where the rich died fast, my grandmother recalled, because they were not used to hard work. She, widowed in her twenties with four little children to rear, knew hard work as a way of life. She survived the camp and fled by foot over the mountains of Hungary by night, trailing behind younger fleeing refugees and catching up by continuing to walk when they rested, thus never resting herself. She walked to freedom. A nephew in Germany saw her name on a list of refugees and took her in until my dad could get her to America. I think that my grandmother's grit and her religious faith instilled in me an appreciation for courage in the face of injustice.

Additionally, both my grandfathers and my father immigrated to America as young men in search of better opportunities. My father, Nicholas J. Holler, left a society where his ethnic background had put him at a cultural and an economic disadvantage and where he had felt the pains of prejudice. He had left Yugoslavia after an earlier world war that also had set anti-German sentiment in motion. When parts of the Austro-Hungarian Empire became Yugoslavia after World War I, the national language changed from Hungarian to Serbian. My father, knowing only German and Hungarian, saw his dreams of continuing school and becoming an engineer die. Learning a new language was daunting in itself, but overcoming the prejudice against Germans and seeking opportunity in a land that favored Serbs seemed more than he could surmount. His uncle helped him get apprenticed as a tailor, and my father took his trade to America. He arrived at Ellis Island as a nineteen-year-old who did not know a word of English. The snickers that my mother occasionally heard when my dad spoke with an accent (an accent quite grand and charming to my ears) cemented my determination to fight the bigotry and intolerance that existed in my own country.

But while I was aware of injustices that my own family members had suffered, I was still unaware of the prejudices and violent discrimination going on against African Americans and other minorities. I was living in America, the "sweet land of liberty," the country "with liberty and justice for all." Did not the Pledge of Allegiance and the patriotic songs we sang in school affirm this truth?

I now realize that as a child I did not live among or attend school with African Americans. But as a child I felt as if I lived in a community rich in diversity. I probably had this perception because my German grandmother lived with us and because I was used to hearing two tongues at home, or more exactly, a mix of both. Variety seemed the norm. Perhaps because of my immigrant upbringing, the four corners of the world seemed meant to mingle. Our family's move from St. Louis, Missouri, to Chicago, a city teeming with diversity and many ethnic neighborhoods, widened my world. In my German/Jewish neighborhood, half of my Brownie troop friends were Jewish, so we celebrated Hanukkah and Christmas together. I was invited to a friend's home to share in the lighting of the menorah. Another school friend was Greek, and a dark-complexioned boy seemed of an Arab or Middle-Eastern heritage. Here also, my child's perception was that I attended a school representing many faiths and ethnic groups, though I later realized that this school also was segregated.

My family moved to the suburbs of St. Louis and Chicago during my junior high and senior high years. There, as I matured, I became aware of discrimination in my neighborhood, and I saw that a disproportionate number of African Americans held lower-paying jobs as maids, custodians, and sales clerks. My older sister and brother-in-law, Elizabeth and Charles Bryan, who were concerned about human rights, helped me voice my concerns. They widened my world politically and culturally through discussions and gifts of books and records, but mostly they influenced me through their example. To be human in the right sense was to seek a just society, they and the rest of my family taught me.

In junior high and high school, I found myself engaged with the concerns of my society through singers such as Bob Dylan, Joan Baez, and Peter, Paul, and Mary and through television coverage. I mournfully watched the funeral of President John F. Kennedy following his assassination. He had been one of my first heroes. I had eagerly read his book *Profiles in Courage* and had vowed to answer his inaugural challenge: "Ask not what your country can do for you, ask what you can do for your country." On the news, night after night, I watched young American soldiers dying in Vietnam or being pulled, wounded, away from enemy shelling and lifted out in helicopters. I thought the war was insane. The boy I went to the junior prom with, a shy, sweet young man who was beloved by his mother and sisters, died in Vietnam. Years later, I found and traced his name on the smooth black stone of the Vietnam Memorial in Washington, D.C. On the edge of my seat, I watched civil rights marches and demonstrations in the early and mid-sixties before I went to college. I felt a sense of outrage at the injustices blacks in the South were enduring and admiration for the courage and determination of the civil rights demonstrators. I remember wishing that I could go to the march on Washington where Dr. King delivered his "I Have a Dream" speech.

At college, I became friends with Marsha, a black student in my dormitory, for we shared an interest in journalism. When Marsha and I decided to room together, we weren't trying to make a point; we simply were friends who enjoyed each other's company. When I told my parents that Marsha and I had decided to be roommates, at first they were concerned. My dad feared that I would lose my own culture and adopt another's. But when I persisted—

the decision had been made and would not be changed, I said—they were accepting and friendly to Marsha. She visited our home along with my other college friends. However, Marsha and I found that some women in our dormitory did not approve of our rooming together. We got looks, as well as a few queries about why we'd want to room with someone of a different race. But I never had to suffer because of my association with Marsha. She had become a good friend of my high school friends who also were in the dorm, and we all ate meals together in the dorm cafeteria and attended church together. In the room we shared, Marsha and I appreciated each other's humor and shared interests, like journalism and music. I loved the Aretha Franklin, Otis Redding, Temptations, Smokey Robinson and the Miracles, and the Supremes that she played, and we would dance as we brushed our teeth, fixed our hair, and got ready to go out on a Friday or Saturday night.

When Dr. King was assassinated, Marian, my other closest black friend in the dormitory, and her black friends shunned me for a while—days, if not weeks or months—and sometimes cast angry, sad, resentful, or bitter looks at me as though I, by being white, were part of the group that had killed Dr. King. At the time, I thought that Marian's behavior was unfair; today, I don't blame her one bit. Marsha never changed. But looking back, I believe that Marsha had to do all of the giving and understanding in her relationship with me, my high school friends, and a few other good white friends we'd made. It never occurred to me to ask Marsha what it was like to be a black student at the University of Missouri at Columbia in the sixties, or to have grown up African American in Missouri in the fifties and sixties. I knew little about her family, whom I had met the day that we moved into our dorm room, nor about their traditions, her hometown, her school days, or, for that matter, about her aspirations. In retrospect, I realized that we seldom *really* talked, though we genuinely cared for each other. I wish now that I had talked more with Marsha about important matters and had further deepened our friendship.

In high school, I had been eager to go off to college and become a hippie. But my high school friend and first college roommate, Barbara, told me: "Marge, you'll never be a hippie. You iron creases in your blue jeans." The hippies whom I most admired also were involved in Students for a Democratic Society (SDS). I frequented the hippie and student-radical hangout, ordering tacos, listening to Otis Redding on the jukebox, people-watching, and, instead of drinking beer, drinking in the conversations of the student radicals. I attended one SDS meeting. I greatly admired the graduate student history major who always wore a gray suit when he led demonstrations. (I later attended his wedding; his bride wore an ERA [Equal Rights Amendment] NOW sign on her bustle as she went down the aisle. Some years later, my friend ran for the state legislature.) At the SDS meeting, one radical said that the middle class, their homes, and their materialistic way of life had to go. I wasn't sure what this angry student meant by "had to go," but I remember how his edict jolted me as I realized that he was talking about my parents and my working-class suburban neighborhood. I began feeling a discomfort with the radicalism I was trying to adopt.

At college I was seeking a means to put my ideas into action. I wanted to influence my campus and my country for the better, but I wasn't sure how to go about it. I did not want to eradicate America's middle class as a student radical. What I *did* want was for Americans to be more idealistic and less materialistic. My impression was that Americans spent an inordinate amount of their lives accumulating wealth and economic security without ever really asking the question, "What should I be living and striving for, not just for myself, but for others as well?" Without a just society, personal accomplishments seemed hollow achievements.

I decided that an answer to social problems might be tolerance and communication between diverse persons and groups, between the power structure and those with demands upon it. Being an optimist, I hoped that if both sides truly understood each other's positions, accord could be reached and fair actions taken. I joined the Human Relations Council, a campus organization that sought to create a dialogue on campus and bring together persons with differing viewpoints on issues. I helped to sponsor forums that brought, for example, administrators and student activists to the same table. I wish that I could say that great strides in understanding and great advances in students' rights grew out of those meetings, but they did not. I also participated in People to People, another student organization that fostered diversity and understanding. I tutored an older international graduate student to help him improve his English, but was incensed when he preferred flirting to learning English, even though he was already married. So much for global understanding.

While an undergraduate in college, I also saw myself as an occasional activist for civil rights. When I demonstrated for one man's rights in Columbia, Missouri, I proudly wrote home to my parents about how I had taken part in a demonstration. I received a letter back from my father telling me that if I participated in any more demonstrations, I'd have to pay for my own schooling. I made a pragmatic decision; I let my parents continue to finance most of my education, though I did attend one or two more demonstrations and joined the silent ranks of an anti-Vietnam War vigil a few times. Once, a group asked if I would help prove housing discrimination in Columbia. I was to look at the places advertised for rent, pretend that I was seeking an apartment, and establish that apartments still were available for rent. My visits with prospective landlords would shortly be followed with visits by African Americans. If they were told that the apartments had been rented, action over housing discrimination could be taken. While my assistance in proving discrimination was real, I never even had to confront the landlords I'd visited. I always was spared the tension and confrontation black people often had to experience directly. And while some progress perhaps was made at integration, the segregated college town full of many closed-minded residents disheartened me. I was beginning to realize the limitations of my liberal radicalism.

Part of my ineffectiveness at producing real social change was due to ignorance. As an undergraduate in the sixties, I was very unaware of conditions for black students at the University of Missouri—what types of discrimination they faced, whether the university actively pursued minority recruitment, what percentage of the student body was black, and so on. Worse, I did not seek to know these things. I was caught up in my own concerns. I have come to believe that unawareness is one of the most pernicious forms of discrimination because individuals often feel that they are not prejudiced and that they even contribute to the civil rights movement when, in reality, they are a major part of the problem by condoning inequality through silence, inaction, and ignorance. I came to realize that as a white American, I have enjoyed opportunities and privileges not available to African Americans.

The deaths of JFK, Bobby Kennedy, and Dr. King left America's youth adrift without a strong leader to steer the course and mobilize their efforts. Some of us sought community and brotherhood in smaller units of society. I and my then husband were drawn to the "back to the land" movement, renting a farm, participating in a food cooperative, exploring meditation and yoga, and strengthening friendships with a few close friends. We thought that if we got close to nature, and if we cherished those we loved, we could somehow start a movement from within that would spread outward. In such a way we would rescue our country from war and materialism.

A turning point in my life came when I worked as a feature writer and editor at *The Kansas City Star and Times* in the seventies and eighties, my second job out of college. Four fellow journalists, three of them black, were significant in prompting me to begin going to church again and ultimately in making a commitment to accept Jesus Christ as Lord of my life. I had been raised a Christian and had attended church regularly before, but I had not had that personal encounter with Christ where I gave my life to him and experienced his peace. At *The Kansas City Star,* my friend Helen was the religion editor, and my friend Gerald an editorial writer. I respected and admired the honest, sincere life that they and a white reporter-friend, Dick, led. They seemed different from other people around me. I visited Helen's and Dick's churches, and later Gerald's, where I first heard the Reverend Jesse Jackson speak. I joined Dick's church, where I was discipled and learned to make Bible study, prayer, worship, and Christian fellowship a part of my life. I later learned that a young black journalism intern at the newspaper had been praying for me, and I now am convinced that her prayers were part of God's plan in drawing me nearer to Him. Thus, three black Christians were instrumental in my receiving the greatest gift of my life, a closer relationship with God. Helen and her husband, a Baptist minister, had initiated the United Prayer Movement in Kansas City whose aim was to bring blacks and whites together over an occasional breakfast or dinner program to share fellowship, be edified by a Christian speaker and music, become acquainted across racial lines, and promote unity in the faith. "Pray for Brotherhood" was the movement's motto.

Working on the newspaper, where I met and interacted with African American, Asian, and Hispanic colleagues and friends, and where I also had two close Jewish friends, allowed me to begin experiencing more fully this brotherhood which I had been seeking. I also played for nine years on *The Star's* women's basketball team, an interracial team that enjoyed fellowship after each game over beer and pizza and that worked its way up from almost the worst in our intramural city league to the best in our age division. My African American friend Gerald was one of our coaches, and our other coach, Steve, another friend to us all, was Jewish. He later married a Roman Catholic on the team. Our shared lives and interests at the newspaper brought warmth, fun, and comfort to those of us working in journalism, a rewarding and challenging, but stressful, profession. Our diversity brought enlightening moments as well. Gerald shared how his family, when rushing their seriously ill father to the hospital in an emergency, had had to go to the back entrance of the Arkansas hospital, the entrance for blacks. A Jewish friend was outraged at the sight of neo-Nazi and Ku Klux Klan members visiting the newsroom. In that moment, this friend felt all of the pain and suffering that these groups had inflicted on his people and others.

As a feature writer, I interviewed people of many ethnic groups and took delight in bringing their stories to the public. In the process, I made friends in the Vietnamese community; and while I could offer some support, information, and encouragement as they built new lives, they frequently enriched mine as I enjoyed their restaurant and grocery store and visited their church to share in the New Year's festivities and to see the dance of the dragon. A dear friend at the newspaper, Laura Rollins Hockaday, also was an influence on my life, for Laura, in both her professional and private life, always valued diversity, brought the community together, and sought to highlight the achievements of minorities in her newspaper columns and features, where she wrote about worthy citizens who had enhanced the quality of life for people living in Kansas City and the surrounding area. Her example rubbed off on many of us.

Just as I sought to bring people together for dialogue in college, as a journalist I saw myself as a bridge or medium between the people I interviewed and the newspaper's readers. The job was satisfying, but with time, I found myself wanting to touch young people's lives more directly. I considered teaching. While in college, I had decided to work for a while on a newspaper and then go to graduate school and teach English. Now, when the newspaper work seemed repetitive and increasingly stressful, appeared to be the time. To test the waters, I did volunteer tutoring at my church and in a local public school. At church, the appreciation and progress of a hard-working young black male student whom I tutored regularly showed me the rewards of teaching. I also became friends with two children I met while writing an education feature story on a program at their Kansas City public school. Their teachers, who felt that they were especially promising pupils, wanted them to apply for minority scholarships at a private school in the city and asked for my help in seeking the scholarships and raising funds for their transportation costs. The young man continued at the academy, while the young woman chose after a year to return to her public school. This young woman went on to study journalism in college and became a broadcast journalist for CNN. I was a mentor and encourager to her because I myself was a journalist. I became good friends with the young man's mother and her circle of friends. We cooked for each other at our homes, where she introduced me to "soul food" at a Super Bowl party; we went to the horse races together in Nebraska; and we shared life's joys and problems, as when her daughter, who had given a speech at school on avoiding teenage pregnancy, later became pregnant herself. My friend, who had raised two children on her own, had wanted to spare her daughter such difficult times. This friend also told me how, while living in Mississippi, she had tried to register to vote but had been blocked several times, once because she could not answer the question: "How many beans are in this jar?" In this friendship, I was doing the listening and talking that had been missing in my friendship with my college roommate Marsha.

I changed careers in my mid-thirties by earning a master's degree in English and becoming a teacher and Writing Center tutor. At the University of Missouri-Kansas City, I quickly learned that the universe comes to the university. I was teaching many international students, as well as older, working students who took classes at night and on weekends to earn their bachelor's degrees. Even among my white male students, I found a diversity of experiences as I observed or they told me of their struggles (alcoholism, difficulty handling anger, and more).

I, a white Midwesterner, found myself daily teaching and tutoring students from all over the globe. I became engaged in their lives, and their concerns also became mine. I marched with my Chinese students to protest the massacre at Tiananmen Square; I paused in tutoring to hear a student from South America share how she had come to the United States after her husband had been tortured and killed for his political beliefs. I looked into the sad dark eyes of a young Afghan woman whose brother had been imprisoned by a rival ethnic group during the Afghan/Soviet war and had never been heard from again. I listened over coffee as a newly married Korean friend shared fears that her husband would not permit her to express her own identity, and I sympathized with a young Islamic student-friend from Malaysia who worried about returning home to an arranged marriage. I also remember the Korean college freshman who knew so little English when she arrived in this country that she translated, word by word, all of her high school texts into Korean so that she could understand the subject matter. Yet she completed high school as the valedictorian of her class! In the Writing Center, we worked together regularly as she tirelessly revised her drafts again and again so that the final essays that went into her freshman English portfolio were near perfect. Hearing such stories and seeing the determination, deep feeling, and idealism of my students could not help but change me. I was struck by the uniqueness and potential of each individual.

While at the University of Missouri-Kansas City, I took a classical and contemporary rhetoric class with Dr. Victor Villanueva Jr., a teacher who has transformed my life as an educator and as a citizen of a democracy. Victor believed that education and dialogue empowered citizenship. In the classroom, Victor modeled his teaching theory, talking with us and introducing us to the ideas of Brazilian educator Paulo Freire, whose adult literacy program brought education and political empowerment to many citizens of his country.

Freire argues that "dialogue cannot exist in the absence of a profound love for the world and for men." Dialogue is an "encounter" between people who permit one another "the right to speak their word" and to participate in "naming the world," which is "to change it" (Freire 76–79). Freire's pedagogy fired my heart as a new teacher and has guided my efforts ever since.

Victor believed in the power of words to bring people together in understanding. Words could avert wars. Words could empower individuals and groups. Words could fight for justice and equity in our society. When Victor became too busy to continue teaching a cluster of weekend and evening courses on rhetoric, composition, and media analysis that he had designed, he convinced me and a professor to team-teach the courses. Soon, I was introducing older white students, some for the first time, to Dr. King's "Letter from Birmingham Jail" and "I Have a Dream" speech, which they saw and heard Dr. King deliver on a video played in class. A few of the men and women were moved to tears by Dr. King's words and presence.

When I moved to Auburn, Alabama, in 1989 to be near family and earn my doctorate in literature, I did not know what I would find in the South. I had my preconceptions. And some proved true. One day while sitting in the student cafeteria at Auburn University, I heard one white male student mention Dr. Martin Luther King Jr.'s name on the eve of King's birthday anniversary. "I'm glad he's dead," the student said to the other young white man sitting next to him. "Me too," his friend answered. But I had many fine, unprejudiced students at Auburn. Not all southerners were prejudiced, and racism was not limited to the South. I remember that when I visited the high school classroom of a friend who taught in a blue-collar Kansas City suburb, a white student sitting near the only black student in the class muttered "nigger"—loudly enough for the whole class to hear.

Hopeful events also occurred in Auburn. Through the initiative of my brother, Dr. Nick R. Holler, a minister of congregational care who is committed to increasing friendship and dialogue between people of different races, my United Methodist Church cosponsored a thirty-six-week Disciple Bible study with an African Methodist Episcopal Zion Church. I was a participant. Sharing God's word through Bible study, song, and prayer was a joy. Our ministers exchanged pulpits, and our choirs sang at each other's revivals. My brother also has been invited to preach several times at the Auburn A.M.E. Zion Church, and we Bible study participants from each church continue to stay in touch.

I arrived at Alabama State University in 1998 a white, fifty-year-old female English teacher. I found my students, the majority African Americans, to be receptive, religious, polite, caring, intellectually curious, and gifted with great potential. My students were friendly and helpful. They offered to carry my bags of books and papers or briefcase from one building to another. When the first student did so, I thought it was a sweet and unusual gesture. Few students had done so at other schools where I'd taught. To my astonishment, a day seldom passed that students did not offer to carry my bags and case. This regular assistance came to symbolize for me their considerate nature. I found myself quickly bonding with my ASU students as I read their life stories in essays or listened as they shared experiences or concerns. Because Alabama State University has a fairly open admissions policy, many of my students arrive at college weak in the basic skills of writing, reading, and analysis, though also capable of keen insight. More of my ASU students have to work, many full-time, to pay school expenses than did students I have taught elsewhere. But if they face more economic hardships, my ASU students also seem deeper, more sensitive, and more mature in some respects because of what they and their families have been through. Many students write or tell of parents who have worked hard to raise them and help pay for their college.

Before I came to ASU, I knew that my students had experienced racial prejudice at some point growing up. But working at an HBCU has taught me how pervasive racism is in our society. As I got to know my students, I learned of discrimination and harassment they had faced. Two young men talked of how police had stopped them and questioned them even though they had done nothing unusual. They simply were black. Their unjust treatment caused by false assumptions reminded me how my journalist-friend Gerald would find older white women avoiding him in the supermarket parking lot when he went to the store in jeans and a jacket. But when he went to the store straight from work in his suit and tie, Gerald commanded respect.

I found myself making some false assumptions also. One of my early students at ASU, although bright and intellectually eager to learn, seemed to distrust me as a teacher and was defensive when I tried to help him improve his rough draft for a writing assignment. Frustrated in my efforts to teach him, I did not understand his resistance and wondered if he was immature, moody, or conceited. Finally, he came to a tutorial session with me to work on a draft. Out of a list of topic choices, he had written on whether he had ever experienced discrimination. He wrote of being one of only a few black students in a white high school and of how a white teacher had assumed from the start that his work would be inferior and how she had belittled his ideas, so that he quit speaking up in class or asking questions. He wrote of how discrimination had kept him from full participation in classroom discussions and learning opportunities at the school because these were dominated by white students and how he knew he was not being fully prepared for college as a result. I realized that he was wondering whether he would receive the same treatment from me. I was struck by the blindness and misjudgment of his white teacher and the white students at that school, and I was thankful that I had been saved from a similar misjudgment. Through his words, I was able to understand how racism can cut like a razor, but seem a mere scratch to the person not under the blade. His essay also helped further illuminate my past friendship with Marsha, my black roommate in college, enabling me to better understand what might have occurred back in the 1950s and 1960s when she was in school. The writing assignment and its outcome, for the student and for me, his teacher, was an example of what dialogue as conceived by Freire could achieve.

In my second semester of teaching at ASU, I assigned topics related to Dr. Martin Luther King Jr. to commemorate his birthday in January and his contributions. I had made similar assignments to celebrate Dr. King's birthday at other schools where I'd taught, and for years I have saved the personal-response writing from one young white male student in freshman English who was awed by King, whom he had never read before, and overwhelmed by his message. This time, I asked my students to compare and contrast the civil rights and opportunities that they enjoyed with those of their parents, grandparents, and other older relatives in earlier times. Or, my students could write on discrimination that they themselves had encountered. I read many "profiles in courage" and encountered unsung heroes and heroines. My students' admiration for their families and their heritage not only stimulated me to learn more about African Americans' contributions to our country, but to learn about my own roots and family and to explore my immigrant heritage further.

For a time after I arrived at ASU, I felt estranged from my own race. I felt as if I were seeing the world through the eyes of a black person. The discrimination leveled at my students and other African Americans became discrimination leveled at me. I keenly felt the injustices that they, their families, and their ancestors had and were enduring, and I felt great anger and bitterness. I believed that if I were black, I would be angry and outraged all the time. When I told one of my black students how I felt, she said that a person "could not live that way." Few white people have contemplated how they would feel if their great-grandparents had been auctioned off or sold by printed advertisement into slavery, working to prosper another family rather than their own. At ASU, as I watched my students struggle to pay for school and books, I clenched my jaw, thinking of wealthy white families who could easily pay for higher education and amenities for their children. The continuing economic disparity in our country is clearly documented.

When I commuted back and forth between Montgomery and Auburn, where I still live with my mother, I felt as though I were coming and going between a black world and a white one. Most of my students and many of my colleagues at ASU were black, and I also was getting steeped in African American culture as I eagerly attended convocations and programs to learn about black history. I perceived Auburn as mostly white because my neighborhood and church were. However, in the last few years, the street on which I live in Auburn has become much more integrated, and a few African American and other minority families and students have joined my church. Therefore, I feel this racial divide less. But more importantly, I see things differently. I see people more and color less.

I identify with my students' aspirations. Often a student will speak of being the first in his or her family to graduate from college, as my siblings and I were. I admire my ASU students for their fortitude in working and attending school at the same time, as we in my family did. When I became an educator, I especially wanted to teach students who had not had all the opportunities that more affluent Americans could give their children. I am sure that my immigrant heritage helped foster my desire to help those "coming up," as one of my students recently described her own experiences. Her family in another city had moved from a dangerous neighborhood to a happy and stable one, and now she was in college, making good grades and working. My older family members knew hard times, too. When my father was just nine years old, he lost his father, who had returned to Europe after earning some money here in the United States. My grandfather, a farmer, had caught pneumonia after retrieving a lost cow from a creek on a cold night. For the rest of his time in school, my father was sent to work on neighborhood farms every summer to help support his mother, brother, and sisters. My grandmother was busy herself, doing other people's laundry before there were electric washers and driers. Her hands would get very chapped. My dad was often hungry, cold, and exhausted. He sometimes was scolded and neglected on the farms where he worked and lived. A kind word or deed was rare and remembered by my father even when he was in his eighties. My mother, Margaret B. Holler, a top student in her class, also had to quit school at the age of fifteen to help care for her mother, who was dying of tuberculosis, and for the rest of the family. Both of my parents would have loved higher education, and both would have excelled. Just as my mother and father gave their children the opportunity to go to college, so I want to do all I can to help my students excel and reach great heights of achievement.

My ASU students are typical college students who often party too much and study too little! Nevertheless, even while bemoaning their immaturity in these respects, I find them to possess character. In fact, I would trust my life with my students. I expect them to do great things for their country, just as their parents and mine have done. My father eventually became the head of men's alterations at men's fine clothing stores and department stores, and in St. Louis he hired the first African American in his shop. Many of my students speak or write of how they want to "give back" to the community when they have good jobs. They especially want to help children and young people like themselves. I feel privileged to help equip them for this task.

At other universities, when I worried about the safety of my students, I worried most about tragedies due to overdrinking and drunk driving, problems typical of college campuses. However, at Alabama State University I also worry about many of my students and their friends and families being the victims of violence in their own communities, or of having to witness things no young person should see. One of my students opened her front door in a high-crime Chicago neighborhood to find a stranger on her doorstep; moments later she saw his face blown away. He had been mixed up in drug deals in the neighborhood. Another student returned from break devastated and stunned by the death of a cousin at a club; her cousin, though uninvolved in the altercation, had been caught in the crossfire. My student, who before was bursting with happiness and the optimism of youth, never seemed the same. The dangers are so imminent now.

Working at this HBCU also has led me into union membership. I am a proud member of the Faculty-Staff Alliance, a local of the American Federation of Teachers (AFT). I waited six months before joining the union. I found that many of my colleagues whom I highly respected were members of the Faculty-Staff Alliance. My union membership has become a significant part of my self-identity, and it also has linked me meaningfully to my maternal grandfather, a German immigrant, who operated the elevator at a coal mine in Peru, Illinois. My grandfather served as treasurer of his local of the United Mine Workers of America, and he and his local helped to campaign for the eight-hour day. In my family's proud possession is a medal commemorating the eight-hour day. The medal reads: "U.M.W. of A., April 1, 1898, Eight Hours. United we stand; divided we fall. In union there is strength." Grandpa Flaig also was elected and reelected township supervisor of Peru in La Salle County, serving for over twenty-five years. During the Great Depression, as township supervisor, he administered the county's relief program for the poor and unemployed.

The faculty at Alabama State University also quickly won my respect and admiration. When I arrived at ASU, I wondered how I, a new white faculty member, would be received by black faculty. I was not worried, for I knew that God would make a way. I found myself warmly welcomed from the start. I respect and admire Alabama State's faculty for their knowledge and their dignity, a dignity acquired through commitment to education and justice.

My department colleagues have become like family to me. We are white, black, brown, Indian, Canadian, Russian, Iranian, and Nigerian, and all participants in American democracy, whose story we are helping to write daily. In my department, a team spirit prevails. I feel cushioned in a caring atmosphere. I find my fellow faculty committed, intelligent, research-minded, humane, supportive, idealistic, and diverse.

One telling illustration of how my colleagues' research has broadened my world is my discovery of an American heroine, Mary McLeod Bethune. Why had I not heard of her when, as a teenager hungry for role models of activist women who changed the world for the better, I had devoured the autobiographies and biographies of such women as Jane Addams, Florence Nightingale, Helen Keller, and Eleanor Roosevelt? Bethune was a renowned educator, activist, and stateswoman in our nation's capital. The answer is clear: African Americans, to our nation's loss, have not been equitably represented in history books and libraries, in literature, broadcast, or print journalism.

And yet, Mary McLeod Bethune can speak to us today in the aftermath of the September 11, 2001, terrorist attack. She can help to guide our country's continuing response to that attack and to threats of other terrorist acts. How we respond might prevent further human suffering and loss of lives in America and the Middle East. Bethune delineates, in her 1947 essay, a lower or a higher road that our nation could take in response to world violence:

"We are approaching a critical juncture in the history of the World, and the destiny of our Nation. One road can take us from suspicion of other nations, to disagreement, conflict and war of unimagined fervors that would blast civilization, as we know it, from the face of the Earth. That road is easy and all down hill.

"The other road," Bethune continues, "is up-hill, tortuous and rocky and only for the strong men to tread. It is the road of national and international understanding, resolving of differences, compromise, agreement and peace, which can lead to fields brighter in promise than the Sun of the Renaissance opened to man.

"Which way, America?" Bethune asks. " . . . As Negro citizens and members of a disadvantaged minority group everywhere we are very much concerned as to what kind of Democracy, what way of life we are to take to the nations of the world. Is it to be the way of the Spirit, or the way of the Sword? Are we to show our strength in guns and tanks—in atom bombs? Or, in food for the hungry, plows to till the field, and in bringing peace to men of good will? Are we to win our way by virtue and persuasion and peace, or are we to shove it down unwilling throats with money and bayonets and war?" Bethune challenges her fellow Americans: "Is it to be the Democracy of the lynching mob and flaunted law? Of intimidation and threat and fear? Or, is it to be the Democracy of law and order, of the 14th Amendment really enforced, of the sanctity of the individual, of the protection of person and home against brute strength and fear?" (Bethune 186–87).

A few of my students at ASU, though they love their country dearly and want to protect it, asked this question in the classroom recently as they inquired how our government can offer blanket condemnations of other nations as evil when our own record of human rights has been sorely wanting, considering America's own legacy of slavery, human rights violations, and continuing racism and discrimination.

As ASU has enlightened and empowered me, so I hope to empower my students. In my teaching, I draw on Henry Giroux's idea of "schools as democratic spheres" and as sites for "self and social empowerment" (Aronowitz and Giroux 20, 43). I encourage dialogue in freshman English and in the humanities course I teach. The humanities course includes sections on ancient cultures such as Mesopotamia, Egypt, Nubia, Kush, China, India, and West Africa, and on Greek, Roman, Hebrew, early Christian, Islamic, and medieval cultures. The course encourages thought on what each culture valued. The course also stimulates discussion on what is to be learned from these cultures and how we are shaped by them. We try to enter into the point of view of the culture being studied to understand its values and methods. During the study of Islam, I invite a Muslim couple on campus to speak to the class and to answer questions that the class may have about the brief readings of the Qur'an found in our course text. Geography professors from India and Nigeria also visit the class. The close look at other cultures causes students to reexamine their own.

I find that when I take a baby step toward learning and teaching about African American culture, I receive immediate rewards not only from my own pleasure and enlightenment, but also from my students' enthusiastic responses and from my increased interaction with faculty and other knowledgeable persons. I also find that one step leads to another, perhaps even providentially, so that I build on what I know. For example, based on recommendations by two black colleagues, I taught Margaret Walker's novel *Jubilee* in my freshman English classes at ASU. The story of Vyry's endurance and victory over slavery and racism, based on the true story of Walker's maternal great-grandmother, captured my students' interest and prompted good discussion and papers, though a few students found the description of slave life too painful. I also found inspiration in Vyry and a better understanding of slavery and the Civil War South. My baby step in teaching Walker turned into surer footing when I learned a great deal about Margaret Walker at my first College Language Association convention. A tribute was made to the late Margaret Walker that year, and at the CLA conference, I viewed a film about the author's life and bought several books of her poems and essays, including a fascinating account of how she researched and wrote *Jubilee*. The next time I taught the book, I could offer my students exciting new background about Walker and her novel.

Additionally, attending two CLA conventions has been nothing short of life-changing for me. The College Language Association is devoted to fostering scholarship by and about African Americans, their literature, and culture. While attending primarily white colleges, I met an occasional black academic; black poets and novelists were invited to my campuses to do guest readings, but to my remembrance, I seldom heard a guest black scholar in the humanities speak. At the CLA conventions, I met hundreds of black scholars—by no means our entire membership either. I heard many of them present outstanding papers and discuss research and scholarly books that they had written. I, a new scholar, was humbled at the quality and extent of their research and writing. Of course, I was working with black colleagues doing similar scholarly work at ASU, but being the minority person at a convention of mostly black scholars drove a point home. I was warmly welcomed as a new member of CLA, but not until my second convention did I learn that CLA was formed in part to provide an academic forum and intellectual exchange for African Americans at a time when they were not welcome at the Modern Language Association and other professional conferences. Yet at its very formation, CLA welcomed scholars of all races.

Over the years, I have come to realize the intersection of literature, the press, and politics. My major professor for my dissertation, Dr. Donald R. Wehrs, introduced me to political and philosophical theorists whose ideas had bearing on the social work of literature. His interdisciplinary approach to teaching English and the humanities helped me fit together religious, political, and cultural aims that I saw not only as compatible, but as mutually empowering for the individual and society. Certainly Dr. Martin Luther

King Jr. saw the complementary spiritual and political force of prophetic utterances such as those of Amos, who declared, "But let justice roll down like waters, and righteousness like an everflowing stream" (Amos 5:24). Justice thwarted was a recurrent somber theme of the prophets, who saw it as their calling to return God's people to equitable dealings with one another. Jesus reiterated this call for love and justice when he identified the greatest commandments: "Love the Lord your God with all your heart, soul, and mind. . . . The second most important commandment is like this one. And it is, 'Love others as much as you love yourself'" (Contemporary English Version; Matthew 22:37–39).

In addition to an interdisciplinary approach to my teaching and research of eighteenth-century writers, English and American, I seek an understanding of how the past empowers the present. Another member of my doctoral committee, Dr. David P. Haney, had me read the work of Hans-Georg Gadamer, who emphasizes "the operativeness of history" in our lives. Gadamer believes that through "bridge building, the recovery of the best of the past" is possible. Dialogue keeps alive past and present thought. Reading and discussion contribute to the formation of a person's thought and feeling (Gadamer 26, 28). Thus, when Frederick Douglass wrote at the close of his narrative in 1845, "Sincerely and earnestly hoping that this little book may do something toward throwing light on the American slave system, and hastening the glad day of deliverance to the millions of my brethren in bonds," he was "faithfully relying upon the power of truth, love, and justice, for success" in his efforts (Douglass 85–86). When Douglass speaks "his word" to our minds and hearts across a century and a half, he participates in naming or changing our world, as Freire terms it, even to this day. When Steve Biko, a student leader and political activist in apartheid South Africa who died in 1977 of a head wound while in police custody, asserts, "I write what I like," his brave words empower us and make us determined to fight injustice too.

I think that I was "called" to Alabama State University. Long before I applied at ASU or learned that it was a historically black university, I would notice the sign off Interstate 85 in Montgomery indicating that the campus was nearby. With wistful yearning, I would glance up at the big brick building on the hill near the sign as I passed by, thinking it must be part of the school. After eight years of graduate school in a college town, I missed the diversity present in a larger city and longed to teach at a city college. Seeing the Alabama State University sign, I felt mysteriously stirred, as though joy and purpose were present though not yet defined or materialized. I now believe that my heart was being called "home," home to the place I belong and where a wise and loving Providence had destined me to work and serve. Called home.

PART FOUR

International

All Welcome

10 / "You're Not White, You're Canadian"

Where I Belong

Jennifer A. Fremlin

I am a white Canadian heathen who finds herself a tenured associate professor of English at a historically black university in the heart of the Bible Belt. I am often asked how I got here, and although I have both a long and short answer, in the end it seems I have ended up exactly where I belong.

I never meant to move to Alabama. Originally from Ontario, I moved to Tuscaloosa in 1986 to spend a year in the University of Alabama's MFA program in creative writing, before returning to Canada and PhD studies. But then I met my husband, who was teaching English part-time, and decided to stay in the program; in 1990 I graduated with the MFA and my husband with his JD. We then moved to the East Coast where I started a PhD program. The plan was for my husband to get his first post-law-school job. But it seemed that we arrived in New England the day the recession of 1990 began. After six months of fruitless job searching, my husband was offered a position as a law clerk in Montgomery, Alabama, which he reluctantly accepted.

Two years later, having completed all of my degree requirements except the dissertation, I joined him in Alabama, and we found ourselves living in a city we had never planned to call home. Our first impressions of Montgomery were less than positive. Searching for housing, we encountered potential landlords who wanted to meet with us in person, and once finding us desirable—i.e., white tenants—proceeded to make not-so-guarded comments about "the kind of people" moving into the neighborhood.

We had been used to living in university environments, having met in Tuscaloosa in a liberal English Department; Montgomery, despite its several colleges and universities, seemed conservative, dominated by capitol politics and Maxwell Air Force Base. When I, a Canadian, opened my mouth in the Winn Dixie or in restaurants or at the Y, I was often asked if I was military, since it was obvious that I didn't hail from these parts. Besides accent, my somewhat different aesthetic sense when it came to clothes, makeup, and hairstyle marked me as a non-southern white woman well before my feminist politics or my outsider's view on southern race relations were voiced. I soon came to feel alienated from this town, and apart from a wonderful independent movie theatre, a couple of good bookstores and a Thai restaurant or two, had little contact with the place. I buckled down to write my dissertation (on race and the Hollywood star system), and within a year gave birth to our first child, a daughter.

Our temporary detour through Montgomery en route to the rest of our lives was by now threatening to stretch out. We were becoming more firmly entrenched in the city's infrastructure: we had doctors, a bank account, season's tickets to the Alabama Shakespeare Festival. I applied at area universities—Auburn University at Montgomery, Huntingdon College, Troy State University-Montgomery—for part-time teaching positions. Accordingly, I taught Freshman Composition for several quarters at Auburn University at Montgomery, an experience that did little to endear Montgomery living to me. The downfalls of being an adjunct are common: no office or telephone with which to stay in contact with students outside of class, low pay, and teaching at the whim of the Director of Composition. But more particularly, several incidents convinced me that I was not in the right place. One day in 1993, for example, I randomly assigned students to work in small groups; when a late student—a white girl from Wetumpka—arrived, I motioned that she join a group. She balked, then refused: the other members of the group were black, and she turned instead to a group that included white students. I was so taken aback at her blatant disregard for my authority that I handled it badly, registering my disapproval merely with a look instead of addressing the issue more directly.

This was not the only time that race reared its head in an ugly way in those classrooms. Most of the time it was more subtle, as in classroom discussions of essays in which race was an issue. It was nearly impossible to discuss *New York Times* editor Brent Staples's assertion, in his much anthologized essay "Just Walk on By: A Black Man Ponders His Ability to Alter Public Space," that being a black man in America caused people to react to him in public places in negative ways, as the white students in the class first wanted to debate whether or not America was really still racist. One white boy went on and on in an essay about how when he and his family attended the funeral of a black woman long in his family's employ, he felt unappreciated and uncomfortable as the only white mourners. I struggled inadequately with comments on the importance of "tone" in writing, failing I suspect to teach him the meaning of "patronizing." In general, I found my teaching experiences frustrating, but they also confirmed my impression that Montgomery was not an environment in which I would ever belong.

Then I noticed a small ad in the *Chronicle of Higher Education:* Wanted, teacher of English Composition, Alabama State University. I applied, knowing little about the place except that it was a "black school." I showed up at the appointed time at the Humanities Department Chair's office. I was introduced to a trim, well-groomed woman, Dr. Kathy Jackson; she greeted me warmly, then dropped to her knees, explaining she was looking for a pink earring. I followed suit, and after we found it together, I began my association with ASU. While we were talking, a typical 3 p.m. Alabama summer thunderstorm erupted: skies darkened, then brightened with lightning, the power flickered, rain pelted down. English majors are taught that Nature's seeming sympathy for human events is a fallacy; and so it would prove to be.

Undeterred by the storm, Dr. Jackson took me to meet Dr. Alma Freeman, Dean of University College, another strong, impressively stylish woman, who asked me point-blank: "Most of your students will be black. How do you feel about that?" I answered that I was writing about race in my dissertation, and looked forward to having conversations that addressed racial issues directly. Next, I gave a teaching demonstration to members of the department who willingly pretended to be freshmen students, hilariously making up fake names for the "Name Game" (in fact, it would be several months before I got their real names straight). Then on to a roundtable interview conducted by a faculty committee, and to the Vice President of Academic Affairs where, following Dr. Jackson's advice, I extolled the importance of correct grammar for college students. And at the end of the afternoon, I began to feel what I hadn't since coming to Montgomery: the possibility of finding a place where I could belong.

When I was hired as a full-time instructor, complete with office cubicle and phone extension, I was thrilled, but also nervous. Growing up in an all-white town in northern Ontario in the 1970s, I'd had little opportunity for contact with blacks; indeed, I still remember vividly our local newspaper's feature article detailing the arrival of our town's first black family, from South America. One of my best friend's parents adopted a black child, whose difference was largely ignored, in the manner of polite Canadians. At the University of Alabama the classes I taught were about twenty percent black; but to me then, newly transplanted from my home and native land, I barely distinguished black and white southerners: they were all American. And so, as I contemplated the job offering at ASU, I was by now more acutely aware of the vicissitudes of white privilege. I wondered how students would respond to a white woman at the front of the room telling them what to read and how to write. But I was greedy, too excited at the prospect of what *I* could get from the experience to let my misgivings keep me from taking the job.

I needn't have worried. Most of the students were used to dealing with white folks, and indeed seemed less critical of my being there than I was. As one student memorably put it, when I broached the subject in class one day, "Ms. Fremlin, you're not white, you're Canadian." We all laughed; but I realized that she had hit on nuances of race and national identity that much more schooled theoreticians had spent careers investigating. Then she added, "Your kids, though—they're white." Moving to Alabama in 1986, I became Canadian; coming to teach at ASU in 1994, I became white.

One of the most significant impacts of being a white faculty member of a historically black institution has been this change from majority to minority status. I appreciate open discussion of a topic that often in "polite company" goes unspoken: race. My second semester I was approached by a faculty member who said he'd heard that I might make a good minority students advisor. At first I was flattered; then I realized that at ASU of course minority students are non-black. For the minority students at ASU, the lesson in sensitivity to race is probably as important as their diplomas. Recently, for example, a white student approached me, upset that some of her classmates did not seem to be extending offers of friendship to her. She said, "They're judging me by the color of my skin." I gently tried to explain that she had always been judged on the basis of skin color; it's only when it is a negative response that she became aware of it.

Although the job requirements were, and remain, daunting—we typically teach four sections of freshman English and/or Humanities per semester, with over one hundred students writing six to nine compositions each in a term—I quickly found that the inherent deadliness of grading so many essays was relieved by the students' transformations of admittedly banal topics into narratives with real power. While I had taught similar classes at two majority-white state institutions, where most of the students are from in-state, Mississippi or Georgia, the diversity of the ASU student body—representing nearly every state and many countries from several continents—produced new takes on old subjects. One student took the topic, "Analyze a process which is of personal significance," and produced an unforgettable account of learning how to swim by being thrown at the age of four into the Caribbean by his older brothers; for him, growing up in Jamaica, such an incident was a ritual redolent of family and culture. Argumentation papers on affirmative action take on a whole new shading when written in the context of *Knight v. Alabama,* which decreed that ASU "desegregate" and actively recruit non-black students in order to receive equal state funding on a par with the University of Alabama and Auburn. When *60 Minutes* did a feature on the unusual court ruling, one student interviewed made the point that forcing HBCU desegregation was historically misguided; as he put it, ASU never *didn't* allow white people to attend, the way that public majority-white universities in Alabama prohibited minority enrollment. Whites just didn't choose to come to HBCUs.

Other familiar readings provoke different discussions than in previous contexts. Staples's essay, for example, earns knowing nods from students who have sadly faced similar treatment at the hands of police officers when driving late-model vehicles, or sometimes by black security guards while shopping in malls around the country. We are now able to get to a point in the discussion where I can point out that Staples's litany is familiar to many African Americans; the fact that his essay was originally published in *Ms.* magazine (once I explain seventies feminism) elicits an understanding of that composition standby, audience.

And I have been able to incorporate my research interests on race and movies into my syllabi; the second-semester composition course has an obligatory research unit, and I soon developed my sections' assignments around topics such as "New Black Cinema," "Blaxploitation Films of the '70s: Positive or Negative?" and "Black Women in Hollywood." The Special

Collections section of ASU's library has plenty of black-culture–themed resources for my students, and not incidentally for my own research, despite the relatively small size of the institution. Of course, not all students choose to write about black-themed topics, and some students I think suspect me of pandering. But most seem engaged in their selections. I show videos on the shift of black roles in Hollywood from the early days until *Soul Food,* and on Hattie McDaniel's achievements in a racist industry. Students have written poems on being black and famous, performed dramatic readings à la Sidney Poitier in *To Sir With Love,* brought Spike Lee's cousin, an ASU professor of psychology, in to discuss Lee's Alabama roots, and demonstrated Jackie Chan-like martial arts.

Not only have the students been hospitable to this Canadian in their midst, but I have found the faculty in the Humanities Department at ASU to be supportive, generous, and sincere in their desire to teach undergraduates. After seeing close up five other English departments in Canada and the United States, where factionalism and infighting were de rigueur, I was struck by the startlingly positive atmosphere in this department. Like the student body, the members of the Humanities faculty hail from many countries and continents and are of different racial and ethnic and religious backgrounds, and yet or because of their diversity, they have crafted a place in Montgomery where all feel welcome. All, that is, who are also committed to valuing human experience and achievement.

Perhaps the most significant experience I've had through my association with ASU is my involvement with our scholars' bowl team, the Honda Campus All-Stars. Upon my arrival at ASU I was quickly conscripted by a colleague who coached the team to moderate at practices, reading questions aloud for the fast-paced game. At his encouragement I auditioned to be a volunteer at the National Championship Tournament held each year in Orlando, Florida, and underwritten by American Honda. For the past seven years I have been an assistant coach of our institution's team, as well as national volunteer, broadening my experience with our team to a nationwide network of hundreds of students from more than sixty-four HBCUs, plus their coaches and one hundred plus volunteers who help run the tournament. Twenty-five percent of the game's questions concern African American culture, which has certainly taught me much about this heritage, but more significantly I feel I have a community that extends to the campuses of historically black academic institutions in dozens of states.

I believe that I am not the only person to become a teacher because I didn't want to leave the classroom—not as a teacher, but as a student. Teaching is a way of staying a lifelong learner, and in the classrooms at ASU I continue to learn. Our students have taught me more about the significance of the experiential and the importance of critical thinking than I'm afraid I have imparted to them. But I suspect that is another truism of teaching: they know us for sixteen weeks; we plunder their enthusiasm and questioning to rejuvenate ourselves. Teaching at ASU has certainly provided ongoing intellectual stimulation if it can keep me excited about teaching rhetorical essay forms. This I think is the most significant aspect of the legacy of ASU, and by extension the HBCU institution: it opens its doors to any and all, without discrimination, creating an environment where all kinds of otherwise disenfranchised intellectually minded people can find a haven. Viewing a recent documentary, *From Swastika to Jim Crow*, about the historical phenomenon of displaced German Jewish intellectuals finding a place, indeed a refuge at HBCUs, brought home to me just how much my personal experience at ASU is part of this bigger picture.

Now, some eleven plus years after finding ourselves in Montgomery, my husband and I have found it to be a more habitable environs than it initially seemed. We have had a second child, bought a house, been promoted. Sometimes I joke that the kudzu is wrapped around my feet, pulling me in and down, that Spanish moss has infected my memories of cold winters, ice hockey, patterns of speech. Canadian identity is often predicated upon negative constructions: you know you're neither American nor British, but just who you are (you ride skidoos and drink your tea hot and slurp maple syrup and know what a curling bonspiel is) is less determinable. I have revised my earlier impressions, and I have come to see that Montgomery is my community, and I must take responsibility for its shortcomings, and work to extol its virtues. ASU is one of them. I no longer see it, as I did that stormy afternoon a decade ago, as an oasis in a hostile town, but as part of that town. For a white northerner, a Canadian heathen, living in the heart of the Bible Belt and, as the tags on my minivan attest, the heart of Dixie, a historically black campus provided the welcome mat, as it has to so many others not originally allowed in the door. It has made Montgomery home.

11 / The Color Brown

An Asian's Perspective

Sunita George

Recently, on a long flight, flipping listlessly through the pages of an in-flight magazine, I came upon an advertisement for a poster on diversity. Beneath a picture of people from diverse racial and ethnic backgrounds was an inscription that read, "Great achievements are not born from a single vision, but from the combination of many distinctive viewpoints." Diversity challenges assumptions, opens minds and unlocks our potential to solve any problem we may face. As I mulled over this all-embracing view of diversity, I wondered to what extent I subscribed to these views, and what my daily-lived experiences have taught me about diversity. Reflecting on the meaning and value of diversity to me, I am aware of how much of the worldview I hold is shaped by my past experiences and socialization. I am reminded that people are, after all, not ahistoric entities. The continuity of events in our lives, and the interpretation of the totality of these events rather than any one event alone, account for many of our deeply held convictions and views. I realize that while many events and circumstances have had a cumulative effect on my outlook and views, my own experiences as a member of a minority group, most recently at a historically black university, have made me more appreciative of diversity.

In my own case, being raised in India where diversity in language, religion, caste, costume, cuisine, and custom is so much a part of life, diversity for me was something I always took for granted. It seems to me that every Indian is a member of some "minority" group or other, depending on how you slice the society. I grew up in the fairly cosmopolitan city of Chennai (known formerly as Madras) in the southeastern state of Tamil Nadu in India. Here I was actually a language minority in the state I grew up in because the boundaries between the Indian states are linguistic boundaries. The kids I played with, the teachers that taught me, and the people I interacted with on a daily basis were all very different from me in terms of their mother tongues, religions, castes, and customs. This was so especially because my family lived on a quiet and beautiful university campus, which, like many university campuses in the United States, was itself a place of great diversity, not only of faculty and students from all over India but also of Europeans and other non-Indians who worked there as well. This residential campus was part of one of India's premier engineering and technology schools, the Indian Institute of Technology, which was established as a joint collaboration between the national governments of India and Germany.

Yet, indisputably, India is first and foremost a Hindu country, and the Hindu way of life permeates nearly all aspects of its social and cultural fabric. Being a Catholic, I was therefore a religious minority in India. As far as I can recall, I was the only Christian student in my class for a long time. Yet, I don't remember feeling, or being made to feel, any different from the other students in my class, partly because I went to a secular school, and largely because such matters do not usually interest children. As a child I remember going to Hindu temples with my friends and receiving blessings from their *pujaris* (priests). I also remember a few of my Hindu friends coming to church with us occasionally, and the skepticism with which a devout Hindu friend of mine regarded the idea of the Eucharist. I suppose to a Hindu, many of whom are vegetarians, the idea of eating the "body" and drinking the "blood" of Christ must have seemed rather cannibalistic! In addition to religious diversity, my friends belonged to diverse castes as well. The caste system has its basis in the Hindu religion, in which members of different occupations were historically assigned to different castes. Later on these occupations came to be performed by families, and hereditary castes came to be firmly entrenched in the Indian society. Americans often ask me what my caste is; I have no caste because, technically, non-Hindus are outside the caste system.

While I was aware of the dominant socially constructed divisions within Indian society, and of my friends and acquaintances as members of these various divisions, non-Indians were, to my mind, the "other" and the "other" consisted of whites, blacks, and other Asians. Therefore about African Americans as a group, I am sad to say, I knew very little at that time. Yes, we were told of slavery in America in our history class, but it was in reference to Abraham Lincoln and the abolition of slavery; we were told of Martin Luther King Jr., but that was always linked to Gandhi and his ideals of nonviolence. As I think about it now, I realize that I never really had a sense of African Americans as a people in a true sense. I don't suppose in those days I was even aware of the difference between African Americans, Africans, and people of African origin in other parts of the world: to me they were all just black. In a way I think we in India were more aware of Africans, and people of African origin from the Caribbean, than of African Americans. There were students from Africa, countries like Kenya, Uganda, Nigeria, and Ethiopia, attending the engineering program at the university, and so the Africans, though few in number, were not so alien to us. People of African descent from the West Indies were familiar through the game of cricket. Cricket to Indians is like baseball to Americans: we are—pardon the pun—absolutely bowled over by that sport. And the West Indies was one of our favorite rival teams. Yet curiously, although I saw Hollywood movies regularly, actors like Sidney Poitier, Harry Belafonte, and Bill Cosby were attached to my mind as blacks without any national affiliations. I enjoyed their movies with a Zen-like quality of enjoying without thinking, and so to my child's mind I did not see them as representatives of a political ideology or a national culture. They were, to me, people who made me laugh or cry or feel a certain way.

My first real encounter with African Americans was, not surprisingly, in the United States, where I came do my graduate work in geography at the University of Georgia (UGA) in 1990. As a graduate teaching assistant, and later, as a part-time instructor at the UGA, I taught a variety of large and small classes. I had only a handful of African American students in my classes. At that time though, it did not strike me as odd that except for one African American student completing his master's program, there were no African American students in a graduate program that was graduating between thirty and fifty students annually. I do not really know why that was so, whether African Americans were not interested in geography, or that the department was not doing enough to recruit interested students. Therefore the first nine years of my life in the United States, I lived in a world that was really quite white. I did have a few African American friends, like the pastor in my church, and a graduate student in physics, but that was all.

A few encounters with African Americans in Georgia stand out in my mind, like the time I went walking with a friend to a quiet black neighborhood. A friendly old man invited us to chat with him. I think he must have been in his late seventies or early eighties. As we got talking, he gave us an oral history of his family, and what Athens, Georgia, was like when he was a kid; he told us of places in Athens I had never heard of where blacks used to be buried; of the white family that used to own his ancestors. He was a good storyteller; he brought to life a time and context that I had only read about in books. Hearing him relate the events in his life in such a matter-of-fact way was a profound experience for me. Although my encounters with African Americans were few and far between, and speak only of a casual acquaintance, they nevertheless personalized a people that I was only beginning to know.

While my life in India had instilled in me an acceptance of diversity, I tended to think of diversity in terms of socially recognized categories, like the religions, languages, and castes of India. Coming to the United States as a student, those categories were soon replaced by two others—race and nationality. Categories, it seems, make it easier to deal with life's diversity. Against this backdrop, my experiences at a historically black university have, in many ways, strengthened my fundamental conviction regarding the need to promote and celebrate diversity. But more significantly for me, my experiences at Alabama State University have challenged some of my own uncritical, and ironically enough, homogenizing views of diversity. I see better now that my presumption that diversity is bounded and defined by dominant socially constructed categories produces an ironic homogenization—conformity within diversity. While it may be hard to take in the entire spectrum of human diversity, I believe we must strive to remind ourselves that categories are merely markers of socially constructed distinctiveness.

Accordingly, the challenge for me at ASU has been to ensure that I do not overlook the diversity and uniqueness of the individuals I meet by pigeonholing them into categories. Diversity as an emblem for variety would mean little without acknowledging the inherent diversity in each and every individual. Margaret Mead, the famous American anthropologist, said, "If we are to achieve a richer culture, rich in contrasting values, we must recognize the whole gamut of human potentialities, and so weave a less arbitrary social fabric, one in which each diverse human gift will find a fitting place" (Mead, 1). Weaving a less arbitrary social fabric requires constant vigilance on our part. It requires, for example, questioning unquestioned categories, challenging assumptions, and thus opening minds.

I applied to ASU in 1999 upon receiving my PhD, when I decided to stay on in the United States. I remember that one of the questions I was asked at the interview was how I felt about working in a black school. The Dean told me that I was going to be a minority, that most of the students were black, and that it was going to be very different from my experience at UGA. In reply to her concerns, I recall telling the Dean about my own background, that I grew up a Catholic in India, and have been a minority all my life, and could not conceive of being a majority in any context. One of the categories that has lingered as a monolith in my own mind is that of "minority." I suspect that I have, at least subconsciously, viewed the word *minority* as a sort of euphemism for the concept of diversity. I perceived diversity mostly in terms of dichotomies—majority/minority; black/white; male/female. Diversity within these dichotomies was something I did not give much thought to. Without discounting certain common experiences, minority as a category could conceal a variety of identities and experiences so diverse so as to render the similarities almost superfluous.

When I first joined the faculty of Alabama State University, where a majority of students are African Americans, I believed, rather naively, that our shared identity as minorities somehow made us alike. Although I still do feel a sense of oneness with my students, I realize also that our vastly different historic legacies provide room for mutual growth and learning. Even common collective historical legacies often reveal different personal experiences; collective historical legacies are interpreted and internalized in diverse ways, and it is at the level of personal interpretations of the African American identity as revealed to me by my students that I find my own understanding and appreciation of diversity becoming more expansive. Just as there is no one and only definitive and singular Asian Indian identity, my students have, more than anyone else, revealed to me that there is likewise, no one and only "true" African American identity either. Therefore I think that to define individuals by categories alone is tantamount to reducing diversity to stereotypes—whether racial, national or ethnic.

Understanding plurality as self-defining rather than something defined by preemptive categories was something that was brought home to me clearly when I read the essays my students had written on geography and identity. As a geographer, I am interested in the extent to which places, or perceptions of places, are an integral part of people's identities. I asked my Honors students, among other things, to describe the different ways in which they would identify themselves, and how that identity affected their sense of place, i.e., what places they felt "comfortable" in and where they felt "out of place." As I read their essays, not surprisingly all but one student identified himself or herself as an African American male or female. And nearly a third of them also identified themselves further as southern African American or African American from the North, and went on to describe in fairly great detail what they saw as significant differences between these two groups of African Americans. Among them, southerners were seen as "more hospitable, warm and moral"; northerners described themselves as gregarious and suave, and a few even thought that they were wiser in worldly matters. There were others that contrasted urban versus rural dichotomies in their identity as an African American. Some of the attributes of people from rural areas or small towns were described in their papers as "boring"; "speaking with a heavy drawl"; and "good moral values." In contrast, urbanites were seen as "fast and having broader multicultural experiences"; "a different style of dressing and speaking."

As an outsider, these were new categories to me. The diversity within my African American students, I am sure, only partially captures the larger diversity among all African Americans. To me it seems then that there are really no self-evident categories, only those that we choose to recognize, and therefore validate, and those we choose to ignore, at least for the present. Identities as a measure of diversity are therefore neither static nor one-dimensional, and I believe we often define ourselves by the context. For example, in a multi-racial context I may be identified as "brown"; in an international context I may identify myself as Asian Indian; in a crowd of Indians I may identify myself by regional affiliations and so on. The larger meaning of what my students' essays signify for me is how they have broadened my own perspective on diversity; I feel strongly that diversity as a concept is best left open-ended.

I do however recognize that such open-ended definition of diversity is hard to implement at a practical level. We simply may not have the time to decipher the inherent diversity of each and every individual that we come into contact with. This presents a dilemma: whether to stick to categories as samples of diversity, or to completely do away with all categories and thereby free our minds of received ideas of differences. In order to get my students thinking about the received ideas behind labels such as black, white, brown for racial groups, I asked one of my classes at ASU to deconstruct racial categories and to outline what in their view was the basis for using colors as defining racial categories. Clearly when we designate colors to different groups of people, we are not strictly referring to the tone of their skin alone (several students in my class have skin tones much lighter than my own, yet I am thought of as "brown," and they, as "black"). I asked my students if colors (black, white, brown) do not really mean just colors, what then do they stand for? One said colors stood for negative stereotypes, another thought that colors represented biological characteristics of different races, and yet another student thought that colors are merely labels meant to evoke a group's collective historical experiences, such as, in the case of African Americans, the history of struggle and freedom and the continuing struggle for equality.

The idea that the essence of collective legacies are captured by colors representing different races led me to ask myself what the collective African American legacy meant to me, and how that understanding has informed my own views on diversity. For me, the collective African American experience of struggle and emancipation has had an almost storybook-like quality, perhaps because I learned of these struggles through history books in India rather than having lived through it. Like many others, I suppose it was a sense of fair play that immediately attracted me to the civil rights movement. Or perhaps I could relate, in some remote way, to what it felt like to be treated unjustly. As I grew older, I suppose, I also recognized in the civil rights movement the potential for other marginalized groups to fight for their civil rights. Undoubtedly, it paved the way for greater acknowledgment, and tolerance toward differences in views and lifestyles, and thereby promoted diversity as an ideal worth pursuing. In my view, the celebration of diversity as an antidote for the cultural myopia of the past owes a great deal to the African American legacy.

I do believe that while the context of these collective experiences may be unique to a particular group, in this case African Americans, the larger experience of struggle—either against an oppressor, or a political ideology, or economic hardships—is an almost universal one; and so is the experience of triumph over hardships. In the particular are often traces of the universal. It is at the interface of this common global human experience of struggle and triumph that the diversity discourse becomes more and more meaningful. I believe that when we share our diverse experiences, looking beyond the blinders of socially constructed categories such as race, ethnicity, and nationality, we may find an overarching similarity in our diversity. This contradiction, of our likeness even in our unlikeness, is, I believe, the cornerstone for any meaningful celebration of our diversity. To me, we do not celebrate our differences merely to show how different we are, but to also acknowledge that despite our differences, we are similar. To celebrate our differences, and to celebrate our shared humanity—that to me is the essence of diversity.

I think that this wider view I have now come to hold has made me more accessible to my students, and less foreign as well. During my first year at ASU, I was constantly looking for creative ways to build a rapport with my students. As a "nonresident alien" in the United States, I was acutely aware of this "alien-ness" (my accent did not help either) and was concerned that this would somehow alienate me from my students. Teaching a world geography class proved to be a blessing in many ways. As a part of the objective of the course, I was required to delve into the cultures and landforms of different regions of the world. When we were talking about the cultures of Asia one week, I was finally asked (after about six weeks of class) where I was from. Then came a few awkward questions about India at first, and soon they were eager to know more about Hinduism—the red dot on the foreheads of some Indian women, veneration of the cow, and a whole lot of other things. Sensing that this was a good opportunity to break the ice, so to speak, I talked about a few customs and traditions of India and also pointed out some similarities between the United States and India, the African American struggle for equal rights in this country and similar such movements in India.

During the next several minutes we discussed the historic commonalities of the civil rights movement in America, and the independence movement in India. I told them how Martin Luther King Jr. was inspired by Gandhi, who was the architect of the nonviolent civil disobedience movement in India's struggle for independence from the British. Many of them wanted to know more about Gandhi and his ideas. Gandhian ideas of self-reliance and conquering one's enemies through peaceful noncooperation, and the power that this message has in overcoming almost insurmountable obstacles, were ideas that resonated well with them.

Later I explained to them the social stratification of Indian society into castes. After outlining the basis for these castes, I told them how historically the so-called upper castes systematically oppressed the lower castes. I told them how the caste-based denial of certain fundamental rights such as freedom, dignity, and equal access to opportunities was very similar to the plight of African Americans in this country before the civil rights movement, in that both systems discriminated against individuals based on ascriptive factors such as race and caste. The similarities did not end there; after India achieved independence, in order to right past wrongs, the government enacted affirmative action programs (popularly known as "reservation"). Much like their counterparts in the United States, these programs were meant to be a means of social and economic retribution for past injustices. And like the controversies over affirmative action programs in the United States, the Indian affirmative action programs have also generated heated debates on the relevance of these programs today, and their effectiveness in ensuring a diverse workplace. Slowly I noticed that the "alien-ness" was being replaced by something akin to acceptance: an acceptance based not on complete conformity, but on the understanding that there are similarities underlying the difference.

As I reflect on my three years at a historically black university, I see how my views on diversity have become more inclusive. Rather than seeing diversity purely as differences between people belonging to established categories, or as differences that necessarily divide people, I think of it more as a fundamental principle of creation. Conventional measures of diversity like race, nationality, and gender are also reflected among the students and faculty on the ASU campus. I remember one of the first things I noticed when I came to ASU was how diverse the faculty here *looked*. In fact, according to the Department of Human Resources Development at Alabama State University, about thirty of our two hundred full-time faculty members are foreign born. The Department of Human Resources Development kindly shared with me the profile of some of our foreign faculty. We have faculty from Europe, Asia, Africa, the Middle East, the Caribbean, and Canada working here. I learned that this record of hiring people from diverse backgrounds was not only a feature of ASU, but was also a feature of other historically black universities (Henderson 1). HBCUs have a better record of hiring faculty from diverse racial and national backgrounds. Unlike other universities in the United States, where minorities are typically hired in such special programs such as Black Studies or African Studies or Asian Studies, at HBCUs, faculty from diverse backgrounds are hired in all disciplines.

This diversity among faculty was, as I have learned during my years here, not merely a diversity of national/ethnic/racial backgrounds, but also of worldviews and philosophies. To me such diversity, particularly in an educational institution, is indispensable for fostering tolerance and acceptance among students—and for expanding their universe as well. My experience has also been that despite the diverse viewpoints and backgrounds of the faculty and staff, there is a genuine sense of community as well, a community that is reflected in the willingness to help and support others. This was revealed to me most vividly when so many faculty members contributed so very generously to help distant relatives of mine who were left homeless after a devastating earthquake in India. This sense of community is at once humbling and uplifting, and for me it provides hope in a world that often seems to have too many divisive forces at work.

In retrospect, my brief time here has, in many ways, strengthened some of my deeply held convictions about the importance of nurturing diversity, but it has also challenged me to look beyond the socially constructed categories of diversity such as race, ethnicity, and nationality, and to adopt a more expansive view of diversity. I am more convinced than ever that the larger goal of the diversity in the end is to transcend our differences and build bridges of community and tolerance toward those who are dissimilar from us in looks, in views, and in lifestyles.

I am curious about the future of the HBCUs in a global era. At an institutional level, for me one of the most admirable qualities of the HBCUs has been their ability to adapt and survive in the face of gross injustices and hardships. And this adaptability is again revealed in the way the institution has responded to calls for diversity. I also wonder at the same time how, in the age of globalization—when diversity in its many forms is almost inevitable—the HBCUs are adapting. Ironically enough, an institution created because of segregationist policies is now in the midst of having to open its doors to everyone. Are we going to see diversity increase to such an extent that the identity of HBCUs is going to drastically change in the coming decades? And if so, what will be the role of the HBCU, an institution founded on the principles of African American identity? How are we going to redefine ourselves? I think the legacy of constant adaptation has equipped HBCUs to handle this new challenge as well.

As I think back to the message on the poster on diversity, I do believe that diversity of distinctive viewpoints and worldviews is critical, if not in solving all the problems we may face, certainly in helping us think about things in new ways. My experiences at Alabama State University have challenged me to reevaluate my own assumptions of what constitutes diversity.

Afterword

John Moland Jr.

This volume presents a collection of personal essays in which the writers as faculty members at Alabama State University describe their experiences in the academic community of an HBCU. Each essay provides an expression of what we can learn from each other in an academic setting that accepts diversity in its faculty and student body.

Diversity of faculty and students on campus and in the classroom at ASU brings a wide range of human experiences and human achievements together in one place. Authors of six of the eleven essays in this book are non-black and referred to as minorities. However, they make it known that at ASU they have found a high level of satisfaction and feeling of welcome as minority members of the black campus community. As one author so eloquently states, the HBCU institution "opens its doors to any and all, without discrimination, creating an environment where all kinds of otherwise disenfranchised intellectually minded people can find a haven" (139). The fallout is a quilted, compassionate community, a comforter held together by respect for one another and the recognition of a common humanity involving civility toward all: that is, taking others into account, so as to exercise respect, fair play, and treatment toward all as human beings.

Historically black colleges and universities have from their inception embraced the concept of diversity both in their faculty and student body, as Professor Jackson attests in the opening essay. This open-door policy was in sharp contrast to that at the white institutions, which rejected diversity by excluding blacks and others. Although the non-black authors express concern about acceptance, given their diversity as minorities at an HBCU, they soon find that the value placed on the human experience of struggle and triumph provides an overarching canopy for all diversity. From this perspective, the composition of diversity at the HBCU institution should not be viewed in terms of dichotomies, nor as a categorical ranking of people, but as a continuum of interrelated relationships, a coming together of human beings in a civil relationship of respect for one another in the pursuit of, and transmission of, universal knowledge. In this context, Professor George, in the closing essay, describes the range of diversity in India and her minority status in India. She also describes how classroom rapport is enhanced by discussing the historic commonalities of the civil rights movement in the United States and the independence movement in India.

It is interesting to note that one of Professor Fremlin's students told her "you're not white, you're Canadian." Although the white professor from Canada and other whites born in the United States are Caucasians, the student may perceive a distinction, not based so much on race, but on attitude, behavior, and relationships. If the student perceives "white" as a way of thinking and behaving, as an ideology held by Alabama whites in relation to blacks, and if Professor Fremlin does not subscribe to that ideology or manifest the related attitudes and behavior, then the student's perception of her is that she is not white. While this is somewhat hypothetical it calls attention to the experiences that this white professor has in her relations with white Alabamians. She finds that many of her beliefs and opinions and her lifestyle and behavior do not coincide with those of white Alabamians. Consequently, she feels somewhat unaccepted at the predominantly white institutions, and in the city of Montgomery as a whole.

The In-Group/Out-Group Paradigm and the HBCU as an Other-Directed Community

The experiences of Professors George and Fremlin bring into consideration the in-group/out-group paradigm involving the concepts of insider/outsider developed by the late Robert K. Merton (351–52). The term *ingroup* describes a group with which people identify and to which they feel closely attached, particularly when that attachment is founded on hatred for or opposition toward another group known as the *out-group*. Members of an in-group feel a sense of separateness, opposition, or even hatred toward those they have designated as members of the out-group. And those of the out-group feel and are perceived as outsiders (Ferrante 133–39). Loyalty to an in-group and opposition to an out-group are accompanied by a strongly held consciousness of us-versus-them. As an outsider, this makes Professor Fremlin feel uncomfortable and rejected.

Professor Fremlin's experiences can also be examined in light of David Riesman's paradigm of the tradition-directed society, community, and people; and the other-directed society, community, and people (Riesman 9–16). The term "tradition-directed," used with reference to personality patterns, reflects membership in a small community based on traditional culture, including traditional authority. Such a tradition-based society constitutes the in-group especially when the rules and patterns of conduct are governed by strongly held convictions as to the proper behavior for all with emphasis on the past and the preservation of the status quo in human relationships. The tradition-directed forces of the Montgomery area seek to preserve the "imposed race-gender biases" noted by Professor Smith (72) and the old patterns of segregation described by Professor Jackson.

By contrast, the other-directed community involves diversity and change, whereby the personality patterns and behaviors of individuals more readily take each other into account in establishing the rules for conduct. Thus, outsiders can find acceptance at the HBCU, as long as they are committed to valuing human experience and achievement, which demands civility in behavior, the expression of respect, and fair treatment. The HBCU is a model of the other-directed community and those involved in the diversity of the HBCU can benefit from the presence of each other and share common human experiences without feeling rejected as outsiders. In fact, the other-directed orientation of ASU, as an HBCU, has enabled it to "survive limited financial appropriations and social neglect" (82), as Professor Markham notes in her description of the qualities found in the "black-eyed Susan"—and survival is prime among those qualities. Professor Franklin emphasizes the need to recognize and preserve the rich history and role of the HBCUs, especially ASU and its "role in sparking the Modern Civil Rights Movement in America" (46). The history of the black experience is an integral part of the history of the making of the United States of America.

The Development of the Other-Directed Paradigm
in the HBCU Community

How is it that Alabama State University evolved as an institution with other-directed community characteristics when other institutions in the city and area did not? My response to that question is that the history of the black experience has been one of diversity growing out of the social construction of the institution of slavery in this country, particularly in the South. The results of the institution of slavery, followed by the institution of segregation, produced the other-directed ethos among blacks and the tradition-directed ethos among whites.

Separateness and dissimilarities characterized the slave's experience in the slaveholding states. Blacks were captured as slaves from different countries and places in Africa with different cultures, including languages and dialects. They were sold and distributed to different places in this country. And, as the slave trade within the borders of this country developed, they were frequently resold and relocated to different places throughout the slaveholding states. In fact, the selling and reselling of the slave was not only profitable for many but also served as a means of maintaining control over the slaves. Fathers were sold away from their children and their mates. Children were sold away from their mothers and fathers. Consequently, there evolved in the black community many aunts and many uncles, many nephews and nieces, and many mothers with sons and daughters who were not blood related but who forged strong ties of relationship based on affinity. In this way, there has always existed in the black community a variety or a diversity of relationships. These relationships of affinity resulted from the tragic experiences of a human social construction, in the form of the institution of slavery. To be sure, there were some slave masters who treated their slaves more humanely. However, that phenomenon was limited and not uniform throughout the slave society, and only added to the diversities and dissimilarities among black experiences.

Given the conditions of imposed diversity and struggle, members of slave families of affinity—and other variations in family type—developed acceptance and respect for each, which provided the social-emotional support that enabled them to cope with their situation together. Surrounded by diversity, captured in a common struggle and plight, the survival of blacks depended upon carefully taking each other into account and exercising civility. This is a major legacy of the black experience and the black family in the United States.

Postslavery experiences perpetuated the diversity, including separateness, through the Black Codes, Jim Crow, segregation, and the southern race/ caste system. Fortunately, some whites, genuinely concerned about the plight of blacks, in cooperation with the persistent effort of black people to promote, support, and provide educational opportunities in their community, succeeded in producing educational programs that led to the development of the HBCU, thereby initiating and adding to the diversity and uniqueness of the black experience. Thus, the diversity of the black experience is captured in the history of the HBCUs, which thereby yield more of an open-group than a closed-group relationship.

The sense of community and togetherness at HBCUs serves as a social force overriding social-economic status and class. In this volume, Professor Moorer's account of his personal situation as a young man from a poor, rural area who struggled to attain degrees in higher education provides a vivid example. For him, the HBCUs "took me where I was and pushed me into becoming a better student" (69). Professor Franklin's account of her family's background and her own career choices provides another example. She is sensible of the privileged social-economic status she holds as "a fourth-generation member of the teaching profession" (50) and feels strongly compelled to serve others in the community, by "educating the 'children coming on'" (49). Professors Smith and Markham introduce their students to lessons in other-directedness, which they draw from the history of the black community, and from their own experience with various black institutions, such as black churches. Thus, the authors of the essays in this volume describe ways in which the other-directed ethos of the black society, community, and people is perpetuated and extended by the HBCU.

The HBCU's other-directed orientation recognizes the presence of the "diverse cultures of America" and perceives diversity as "one of America's greatest assets," as Professor Jones puts it (41). Professor Ely, a minority midwestern male, writes that "Alabama State University has allowed me to pursue my life with dignity, purpose, and meaning" (100). Commenting on the diversity at ASU, Professor Stephens, who is of German ancestry, writes that "My department colleagues have become like family to me" (125). Similarly, Professor Westhauser, a Yankee of European descent, was adopted as a "play-father" by one of his black students and now calls ASU his "home" (103, 109). As Professor Stephens goes on to say, "We are white, black, brown, Indian, Canadian, Russian, Iranian, and Nigerian, and all participants in American democracy, whose story we are helping to write daily" (125–26).

Conclusion

Let me close by emphasizing important aspects of the in-group/out-group paradigm and the tradition-directedness/other-directedness paradigm for diversity and community on the HBCU campus.

The history of the black experience has been and is one of diversity and that diversity is reflected in the HBCU. The presence of genuine diversity on the HBCU campus allows for inclusion. Diversity allows for acceptance and is essential in the pursuit of knowledge. The in-group/out-group concept loses its grasp in the midst of diversity. The acceptance-rejection concept loses its grasp in the midst of diversity. The we/they, them/us syndrome loses its grasp in the midst of diversity. The cement, the glue if you will, for the campus community, in the presence of genuine diversity, involves valuing the human experience, its struggles and achievements.

The in-group, tradition-directed institution, by focusing on the us/them syndrome, functions as the closed society, restricting movement, restricting acceptance of others. The closed society is turned inward in keeping with the tradition-oriented society described by David Riesman. The closed society is traditional, self-oriented, stagnated, and rejects interaction with others, and is egoistic, that is, expressing and holding to a doctrine of self-interest. The HBCU community as the open society is characterized by uncorrupted diversity; it encourages movement and the acceptance of others; it values human experiences and human achievements. The HBCU community, because of its diversity, is open to change and the broader understanding of universal human experiences, and universal human achievements, that provide for an other-oriented worldview.

Appendix: America's Historically Black Colleges and Universities*

1. Alabama A&M University; Normal, AL
2. Alabama State University; Montgomery, AL
3. Albany State University; Albany, GA
4. Alcorn State University; Lorman, MS
5. Allen University; Columbia, SC
6. Arkansas Baptist College; Little Rock, AR
7. Atlanta Metropolitan College; Atlanta, GA
8. Barber-Scotia College; Concord, NC
9. Benedict College; Columbia, SC
10. Bennett College; Greensboro, NC
11. Bethune-Cookman College; Daytona Beach, FL
12. Bishop State Community College; Mobile, AL
13. Bluefield State College; Bluefield, WV
14. Bowie State University; Bowie, MD
15. Central State University; Wilberforce, OH
16. Charles R. Drew University of Medicine and Science; Los Angeles, CA
17. Cheyney University of Pennsylvania; Cheyney, PA
18. Chicago State University; Chicago, IL
19. Claflin College; Orangeburg, SC
20. Clark Atlanta University; Atlanta, GA
21. Clinton Junior College; Rock Hill, SC
22. Coahoma Community College; Clarksdale, MS
23. Compton Community College; Compton, CA
24. Concordia College; Selma, AL

25. Coppin State College; Baltimore, MD
26. Cuyahoga Community College; Cleveland, OH
27. Delaware State University; Dover, DE
28. Denmark Technical College; Denmark, SC
29. Dillard University; New Orleans, LA
30. J. F. Drake State Technical College; Huntsville, AL
31. Edward Waters College; Jacksonville, FL
32. Elizabeth City State University; Elizabeth City, NC
33. Fayetteville State University; Fayetteville, NC
34. Fisk University; Nashville, TN
35. Florida A&M University; Tallahassee, FL
36. Florida Memorial College; St. Augustine, FL
37. Fort Valley State College; Fort Valley, GA
38. Grambling State University; Grambling, LA
39. Hampton University; Hampton, VA
40. Harris-Stowe State College; St. Louis, MO
41. H. Councill Trenholm State Technical College; Montgomery, AL
42. Hinds Community College-Utica Campus; Utica, MS
43. Howard University; Washington, DC
44. Huston-Tillotson College; Austin, TX
45. Interdenominational Theological Center; Atlanta, GA
46. Jackson State University; Jackson, MS
47. Jarvis Christian College; Hawkins, TX
48. Johnson C. Smith University; Charlotte, NC
49. Kennedy-King College; Chicago, IL
50. Kentucky State University; Frankfort, KY
51. Knoxville College; Knoxville, TN
52. Lane College; Jackson, TN
53. Langston University; Langston, OK
54. Lawson State Community College; Birmingham, AL
55. LeMoyne-Owen College; Memphis, TN
56. Lewis College of Business; Detroit, MI
57. Lincoln University of Missouri; Jefferson City, MO
58. Lincoln University of Pennsylvania; Lincoln University, PA
59. Livingstone College and Hood Theological Seminary; Salisbury, NC
60. Martin University; Indianapolis, IN
61. Mary Holmes College; West Point, MS
62. Medgar Evers College; Brooklyn, NY
63. Meharry Medical College; Nashville, TN
64. Miles College; Birmingham, AL

65. Mississippi Valley State University; Itta Bena, MS
66. Morehouse College; Atlanta, GA
67. Morehouse School of Medicine; Atlanta, GA
68. Morgan State University; Baltimore, MD
69. Morris Brown College; Atlanta, GA
70. Morris College; Sumter, SC
71. New York City Technical College; Brooklyn, NY
72. Norfolk State University; Norfolk, VA
73. North Carolina A&T State University; Greensboro, NC
74. North Carolina Central University; Durham, NC
75. Oakwood College; Huntsville, AL
76. Paine College; Augusta, GA
77. Paul Quinn College; Dallas, TX
78. Philander Smith College; Little Rock, AR
79. Prairie View A&M University; Prairie View, TX
80. Rust College; Holly Springs, MS
81. Saint Augustine's College; Raleigh, NC
82. Saint Paul's College; Lawrenceville, VA
83. Savannah State University; Savannah, GA
84. Selma University; Selma, AL
85. Shaw University; Raleigh, NC
86. Shelton State Community College; Tuscaloosa, AL
87. Shorter College; North Little Rock, AR
88. Simmons University Bible College; Louisville, KY
89. Sojourner-Douglass College; Baltimore, MD
90. South Carolina State University; Orangeburg, SC
91. Southern University and A&M College; Baton Rouge, LA
92. Southern University at New Orleans; New Orleans, LA
93. Southern University at Shreveport-Bossier City; Shreveport, LA
94. Southwestern Christian College; Terrell, TX
95. Spelman College; Atlanta, GA
96. Stillman College; Tuscaloosa, AL
97. Talladega College; Talladega, AL
98. Tennessee State University; Nashville, TN
99. Texas College; Tyler, TX
100. Texas Southern University; Houston, TX
101. Tougaloo College; Tougaloo, MS
102. Tuskegee University; Tuskegee, AL
103. University of Arkansas at Pine Bluff; Pine Bluff, AR
104. University of the District of Columbia; Washington, DC

105. University of Maryland, Eastern Shore; Princess Anne, MD
106. University of the Virgin Islands; St. Thomas, Virgin Islands
107. Virginia State University; Petersburg, VA
108. Virginia Union University; Richmond, VA
109. Virginia University of Lynchburg; Lynchburg, VA
110. Voorhees College; Denmark, SC
111. Wayne County Community College; Detroit, MI
112. West Virginia State College; Institute, VA
113. Wilberforce University; Wilberforce, OH
114. Wiley College; Marshall, TX
115. Winston-Salem State University; Winston-Salem, NC
116. Xavier University of Louisiana; New Orleans, LA
117. York College (The City of New York); Jamaica, NY

*2004 members of the National Association for Equal Opportunity in Higher Education, an organization of HBCUs founded in 1969.

Bibliography

Works Cited

"Alabama State University: The History." *The Inauguration of President Joe A. Lee.* Montgomery: Alabama State University, 2003.

Angelou, Maya. *Wouldn't Take Nothing for My Journey Now.* New York: Random House, 1993.

Aronowitz, Stanley, and Henry A. Giroux. *Education under Siege: The Conservative, Liberal, and Radical Debate over Schooling.* South Hadley, MA: Bergin & Garvey, 1985.

Auburn University. *www.ocm.auburn.edu/toppage/aboutauburn/briefhistory.html.* February 7, 2004.

Bennett, Lerone Jr. *Before the Mayflower: A History of Black America.* 5th ed. New York: Penguin Books, 1984.

Bethune, Mary McLeod. *Building a Better World,* ed. Audrey Thomas McCluskey and Elaine M. Smith. Bloomington: Indiana University Press, 1999.

Brown University. *Brown.* Volume 12, Number 5 (November 1983). Providence, RI: Brown University.

Button, H. Warren, and Eugene F. Provenzo Jr. *History of Education and Culture in America.* Englewood Cliffs, NJ: Prentice-Hall, 1983.

Caver, Joseph. "Marion to Montgomery: A Twenty Year History of Alabama State University 1867–1887." MA Thesis. Montgomery: Alabama State University, 1982.

Cornell University. *www.cornell.edu/CUHomePage/Mission.html.* February 7, 2004.

Delmarva Business League. http://skipjack.net/le_shore/dbl/dbl_home.htm. August 30, 2004.

Department of the Interior. "Historically Black Colleges and Universities." www.doi.gov/hrm/black.html. February 26, 2004.

Douglass, Frederick. *Narrative of the Life of Frederick Douglass, An American Slave. Written by Himself.* Boston: Published at the Anti-Slavery Office, 1845. In *The Frederick Douglass Papers, Series Two, Autobiographical Writings. Vol. 1. Narrative,* ed. John W. Blassingame, John R. McKivigan, and Peter P. Hinks; Gerald Fulkerson, textual ed. New York: Yale University Press, 1999.

Fauset, Jessie. "The Thirteenth Biennial of the N.A.C.W." *Crisis* (October 1922): 260.

Ferrante, Joan. *Sociology—the United States in a Global Community.* Belmont, CA: Wadsworth, 1995.

Freeman, Kassi, ed. *African American Culture and Heritage in Higher Education Research and Practice.* Westport, CT: Praeger, 1998.

Freire, Paulo. *Pedagogy of the Oppressed,* trans. Myra Bergman Ramos. New York: Seabury Press, 1970.

Friedan, Betty. *The Feminine Mystique.* New York: Dell, 1983.

Frost, Robert. "The Road Not Taken." In *Complete Poems of Robert Frost.* New York: Holt, 1968.

Gadamer, Hans-Georg. "On the Scope and Function of Hermeneutical Reflection (1967)," trans. G. B. Hess and R. E. Palmer. In *Philosophical Hermeneutics,* trans. and ed. David E. Linge. Berkeley: University of California Press, 1976. 18–43.

Galegroup. "Coretta Scott King." *www.galegroup.com/free resources/whm/bio/king_c_s.htm.* May 25, 2003.

Gray, Fred D. *Bus Ride to Justice: Changing the System by the System.* Montgomery, AL: Black Belt Press, 1995.

Harlan, Louis R. *Booker T. Washington: The Making of a Black Leader 1856–1901.* New York: Oxford University Press, 1972.

Healy, P. "Black College Struggles with Court Order that it Recruit Whites." *Chronicle of Higher Education* 42: 22 (February 9, 1996): A28.

Henderson, Theresa. "Faculty Salaries at Historically Black Institutions Stuck in Slump." *University Faculty Voice* 8:1. September 2003: 1+.

"History of Alabama State University." *Hornet Tribune.* February 9, 2001. n.p.

Interview with G. Garrick Hardy. *Montgomery-Tuskegee Times* September 6, 1979: 7.

Jackson, Cynthia L. *African American Education: A Reference Handbook.* Santa Barbara, CA: ABC-CLIO, 2001.

Jaschik, S. "Alabama Desegregation: Federal Judge Says the State's Two Public Black

Universities Must Become Less So." *Chronicle of Higher Education* 41: 48 (August 11, 1995): A21–A22.

Jordan, Winthrop D. *White over Black: American Attitudes toward the Negro 1550–1812.* New York: for the Institute of Early American History and Culture by W. W. Norton, 1977.

Kidd, Sue Monk. "A Penguin Reader's Guide to *The Secret Life of Bees.*" In *The Secret Life of Bees.* New York: Penguin, 2002. 1–15.

King, Martin Luther, Jr. *The Autobiography of Martin Luther King, Jr.,* ed. Clayborne Carson. New York: Warner Books, 1998.

———. "I Have a Dream." In *A Call to Conscience: The Landmark Speeches of Dr. Martin Luther King, Jr.,* eds. Clayborne Carson and Kris Shepard. New York: Intellectual Property Management with Warner Books, 2001.

———. *Stride toward Freedom: The Montgomery Story.* New York: Harper, 1958.

Lerner, Gerda. *Black Women in White America: A Documentary History.* New York: Vintage, 1972.

Litwack, Leon F. *Trouble in Mind: Black Southerners in the Age of Jim Crow.* New York: Vintage Books, 1999.

"Martin Luther King." *www.nobel.se/peace/laureates/1964/king-bio.html.* May 25, 2003.

Mayberry, Katherine J., ed. *Teaching What You're Not: Identity Politics in Higher Education.* New York: New York University Press, 1996.

McGrath, Earl J. *The Predominantly Negro Colleges and Universities in Transition.* New York: Bureau of Publications, Teachers College, Columbia University, 1965.

Mead, Margaret. "Margaret Mead Quotes." www.brainyquote.com/quotes/quotes/margaretme132704.html.

Merton, Robert K. *Social Theory and Social Structure.* New York: The Free Press, 1968.

Meyer, Adolphe Erich et al. "History of Education." *New Encyclopaedia Britannica.* 15th ed. 2002.

National Association for Equal Opportunity in Higher Education. www.nafeo.org/members.html.

Norton, Mary Beth, David M. Katzman, Paul D. Escott, Howard P. Chudacoff, Thomas G. Paterson, and William M. Tuttle, Jr. *A People and a Nation. A History of the United States.* 2nd ed. Boston: Houghton Mifflin, 1986.

"Origins of the State Federation of Colored Women's Clubs." *The Colored Alabamian* [Montgomery]. July 25, 1908: 3.

Parsons, Michael D. *Power and Politics: Federal Higher Education Policymaking in the 1990s.* Albany: State University of New York Press, 1997.

Paterson, Judith Hillman. "To Teach the Negro." *Alabama Heritage* (Spring 1996): 6–17.

Riesman, David. *The Lonely Crowd: A Study of the Changing American Character.* New Haven, CT: Yale University Press, 1950.

Robinson, Jo Ann. *The Montgomery Bus Boycott and the Women Who Started It: The Memoir of Jo Ann Robinson,* ed., with a foreword, by David J. Garrow. Knoxville: University of Tennessee Press, 1987.

Roebuck, Julian B., and K. S. Murty. *Historically Black Colleges and Universities: Their Place in American Higher Education.* Westport, CT: Praeger, 1993.

Seay, Solomon S. *I Was There by the Grace of God.* Montgomery, AL: The Seay Foundation, 1990.

Simmons, Gloria M., and Helene D. Hutchinson. *Black Culture: Reading and Writing Black.* New York: Holt, Rhinehart and Winston, 1972.

Smith, Elaine M. "Mary McLeod Bethune and the National Youth Administration." In *Clio Was a Woman: Studies in the History of American Women,* ed. Mabel E. Deutrich and Virginia C. Purdy. Washington DC: Howard University Press. 149–177.

"Special Presentations." In the St. John's AME Church Worship Service celebrating "A Century of Service" of the St. John's Working Club. Video. May 27, 2001.

University of Alabama. "A Brief History of the University of Alabama." www.ua.edu/history.html. February 24, 2004.

Washington, Booker T. "Up from Slavery." In *Call and Response: The Anthology of the African American Experience,* eds. Patricia Liggens Hill et al. Boston: Houghton Mifflin, 1998. 660–88.

Watkins, Levi. *Fighting Hard: The Alabama State Experience.* Detroit: Harlo Press, 1987.

Wells, Ida B. *Crusade for Justice: The Autobiography of Ida B. Wells,* ed. Alfreda M. Duster. Chicago: Chicago University Press.

Westhauser, Karl E. "Revisiting the Jordan Thesis: 'White over Black' in Seventeenth-Century England and America." *Journal of Negro History* 85:3 (Summer 2000): 112–22.

Woodson, Carter Godwin. *The Mis-Education of the Negro.* 1933. Trenton, NJ: African World Press, 1990.

Further Reading

Bacote, Clarence A. *The Story of Atlanta University: A Century of Service 1865–1965.* Princeton, NJ: Princeton University Press, 1969.

Barber Sr., Richard E. *The Economic Emancipation of African Americans.* Somerset, NJ: Penny Lovers of America, 1990.

Bowman, J. Wilson. *America's Black and Tribal Colleges.* South Pasadena, CA: Sandcastle, 1994.

Brawley, James P. *Two Centuries of Methodist Concern: Bondage, Freedom and Education of Black People.* New York: Vantage, 1974.

Garibaldi, Antoine, ed. *Black Colleges and Universities: Challenges for the Future.* New York: Praeger, 1984.

Hacker, Andrew. *Two Nations: Black and White, Separate, Hostile, Unequal.* New York: Ballantine, 1995.

Hill, Susan. *The Traditionally Black Institutions of Higher Education, 1860 to 1982.* Washington DC: U.S. Department of Education, 1985.

Jones, Ann. *Uncle Tom's Campus.* New York: Praeger, 1973.

LeMelle, Tilden J., and Wilbert J. LeMelle. *The Black College: A Strategy for Achieving Relevancy.* New York: Praeger, 1969.

Merton, Robert K. "Insiders and Outsiders: A Chapter in the Sociology of Knowledge." *American Journal of Sociology* 78 (July 1972): 9–47.

Moody, Ann. *Coming of Age in Mississippi.* New York: Dial Press, 1968.

Paterson, Judith Hillman. *Sweet Mystery: A Book of Remembering.* Tuscaloosa: University of Alabama Press, 2001.

Price, Gregory N. "The Idea of a Historically Black University." *Negro Educational Review* 51:3–4 (July-October 2000): 99–113.

Sims, Serbrenia J. *Diversifying Historically Black Colleges and Universities: A New Higher Education Paradigm.* Westport, CT: Greenwood, 1994.

Willie, Charles V., and Ronald R. Edmonds, eds. *Black Colleges in America: Challenge, Development, Survival.* New York: Teacher's College Press, 1978.

Contributors

Volume Editors, from left to right, Jennifer Fremlin, Karl Westhauser, and Elaine Smith.

JENNIFER A. FREMLIN joined the faculty of Alabama State University in 1994 and is Associate Professor of English and Humanities. Born and raised in Canada, she earned a BA in English from York University and an MA in English from Carleton University before moving to Tuscaloosa, Alabama, where she earned an MFA in fiction writing. She is a coauthor of *Writing with Class,* a composition textbook, and author of several stories published in Canada and the United States.

KARL E. WESTHAUSER joined the faculty of Alabama State University in 1993 and is Associate Professor of History. He is a native of New York City and Phi Beta Kappa from Cornell University, where he earned a BA in history. He earned his MA and PhD in history from Brown University.

ELAINE M. SMITH joined the faculty of Alabama State University in 1976. A Florida native, she grew up in Daytona Beach on the campus of Bethune-Cookman College, where she earned a BA in history. She earned an MA in history from Boston University. She is Editorial Advisor to the largest microfilm editions of the *Mary McLeod Bethune Papers* and coeditor of *Mary McLeod Bethune: Building a Better World* (1999).

Janice Franklin, Viriginia Jones, and Kathy Dunn Jackson.

JANICE R. FRANKLIN joined the faculty of Alabama State University in 1978 and is Director of Library and Learning Resources and founding Director of the National Center for the Study of Civil Rights and African-American Culture. A native of Montgomery, Alabama, she earned a BS in sociology, with a minor in psychology, from Tuskegee Institute. She earned an MSLS from Atlanta University and a PhD in library and information studies from Texas Woman's University. She is the author of *Database Ownership and Copyright Issues among Automated Library Networks.*

VIRGINIA M. JONES joined the faculty of Alabama State University in 1981 and is Professor of English and Humanities. Raised in Birmingham, Alabama, she entered the Sacred Heart Convent in Cullman, Alabama, where she earned her BA in English from Benedictine College (Atchison, Kansas). After leaving the convent, she served as a youth minister in Atlanta, Georgia, and earned an MA in English and a PhD in modern American literature from Georgia State University. She is a co-author of *Writing with Class,* a composition textbook.

KATHY DUNN JACKSON joined the faculty of Alabama State University in 1964 and retired as Professor of English and Humanities in 1998. A native of Montgomery, Alabama, she attended ASU's nursery/kindergarten and elementary, junior high, and high schools. She received a BA from Fisk University, an MA from the University of Michigan, and an EdD from Auburn University.

Annie Pearl Markham, Sunita George, and Frank Moorer.

ANNIE P. MARKHAM teaches courses in African American Humanities and English and joined the faculty of Alabama State University in 1987. A Mississippi native, she earned a BS from Jackson State University and an MEd from Mississippi College. She is a coauthor of *Writing with Class,* a composition textbook.

SUNITA GEORGE joined the faculty of Alabama State University in 1999 and is Associate Professor of Geography. Born and raised in Chennai (formerly, Madras), India, she earned an MA and a PhD in geography from the University of Georgia. She is a coauthor of *Fundamentals of World Geography,* a college-level textbook.

FRANK E. MOORER joined the faculty of Alabama State University in 1994 and is Associate Professor of Humanities. A native of Pink's Bottom, Alabama, in rural Dallas County, he attended one-room Pine Top Elementary, graduated from R. B. Hudson High School in Selma, Alabama, in 1957, then attended Oakwood College for two years. He earned a BA from Rust College, an MS in library service from the Atlanta University School of Library Service, and an MA and a PhD in American studies from the University of Iowa. He is coeditor of *Richard Wright: A Collection of Critical Essays.*

Robert Ely, Margaret Stephens, and John Moland.

ROBERT ELY joined the faculty of Alabama State University in 1977 and is Associate Professor of English and Humanities. He grew up in Indiana and was educated there, earning a BA and an MA in English from Manchester College. He earned a doctor of jurisprudence from Indiana University and is licensed to practice law in Alabama. He is coauthor, with T. Clifford Bibb, of *The Humanities: A Cross-Cultural Approach,* and author of two books of poetry, *Mose T's Slapout Family Album* and *Encanchata.*

MARGARET HOLLER STEPHENS joined the faculty of Alabama State University in 1998 as Assistant Professor of English and Humanities. She earned her BA in journalism from the University of Missouri, Kansas City, and her MA and PhD in English from Auburn University. She has been a feature writer and editor for the *Kansas City Star and Times* and is a coauthor of *Writing with Class,* a composition textbook.

JOHN MOLAND JR. joined the faculty of Alabama State University as Professor of Sociology in 1988 and retired as Chair of the Department of History and Social Science in 2000. He earned a BA and an MA in sociology from Fisk University and a PhD in sociology from the University of Chicago. He served as principal investigator and director of research, training, and development projects in Kenya, Tanzania, Sierra Leone, and elsewhere. He is past president of the American Sociological Association's Race and Ethnic Minorities Section and of the Southern Sociological Society.

Index

Father Purcell Memorial Center for Exceptional Children, 78
Fauset, Jessie, 77
Finley, Peyton, 6, 21
First Baptist Church, 30, 68
First Congregational Church, 75
Fisk University, viii, 29, 31, 66, 79, 168, 170
Fort Sumter, 106
Franklin, Aretha, 114
Franklin, Janice R., viii, 44–52, 153, 155, 168 (photo)
Franklin, John Hope, 46
Frasier, Paris, 89 (photo)
Freedmen's Bureau, 5–6, 21
Freedom Riders, 29–30, 36
Freedom Rides, 31
Freeman, Alma, 39, 135
Freire, Paulo, 120, 122, 129
Fremlin, Jennifer A., x, 133–139, 151, 152, 153, 167 (photo)
Friedan, Betty, 7
From Swastika to Jim Crow, 139
Frost, Robert, 98

Gadamer, Hans-Georg, 129
Gamble, Harold, 89 (photo)
Gandhi, Mohandas, 104, 142, 147–48
George, Sunita, x, 140–50, 152, 169 (photo)
Georgia, University of, 142, 169
Georgia State University, 38, 168
Gibbs, Henrietta M., 78
Giddings, Elder, 60
Gilmore, Mark, 31
Girl Scouts, 76
Giroux, Henry, 127
Glass, Arthur and Mrs., 30
Glass, Thelma, 71
God, 48, 67, 71, 74, 104–5, 110, 111, 117, 121, 125, 129
Go Tell It on the Mountain, 37
Gray, Fred, 9
Great Society, 10–11, 14
Green, Carver, 89 (photo)
Griffin (schools superintendent), 63
Grisby, Lucy Clemmons, 69

Hall, Prince, 3
Hamlet, 68
Hampton Institute, 7
Hampton University, 7
Handel, George Friedrich, *Messiah,* 58
Haney, David P., 129
Hansberry, Lorraine: *A Raisin in the Sun,* 64
Hardy, John Garrick, 48–49
Hardy, Johnelia, 89 (photo)
Harper, Consuelo, 76
Harris, William, 44
Harrison (teacher), 55
Hartford Seminary, 66
Harvard University, 1–2, 8, 98
Harvey, Murray, Sr., 59
Hayes, Roland, 22
Head Start, Project, 11
Heart of Dixie, 139
Herring, Patricia Ann, 89 (photo)
Higher Education Act (1965), 8; Title III of, 12; Title IV of, 11; Title IX of, 13
Hindu religion, 141, 147
Historically black colleges and universities (HBCUs), i, vii, 1, 15–16, 136, 137, 140, 143; and African diaspora, 57; and civil rights movement, 51, 57, 65, 66, 68–69; and ingroup/outgroup paradigm, 152; as model of "other-directed" community, 152; as network, 138; as strongholds of black community, 7, 47; commitment to, 81–83, 97–98; cultural opportunities provided by, 21–25, 33, 40–41, 46, 58, 64; debt owed to, 49, 69; diversity characteristic of, 139, 148–50, 151–52, 155; encourage student achievement, 57, 58, 60, 65–66, 67, 69, 99, 103, 121–22, 155; extend "other-directed" ethos of black community, 155; inform students of heritage, 33, 40–41, 47, 49–50, 147–48; mission of, ix, 50; opportunities for personal growth provided by, 38–40, 42, 57–61, 64, 65, 66, 68, 100, 144, 149; preservation of, 48; preserve black history, 49–50, 51–52, 68, 155; provide hands-on teaching, 60, 87–88, 103, 122, 147; and teacher education, 44,